The Tennis Bubble

Educating Tennis:

a few years in the life of an emerging tennis star

by Richard Bonte

The Tennis Bubble, Copyright, 2011, 2021
Richard Bonte. All rights reserved.

ISBN Number: 978-1-4709-9322-1
e-ISBN Number: 978-1-4709-9318-4

TABLE OF CONTENTS

The Tennis Bubble

ACKNOWLEDGEMENTS

To *Alessandra*, my daughter, without whom this book wouldn't have been possible. It is she who came up with the title, "The Tennis Bubble." Although she and I don't agree with many of the conclusions I've drawn here, she was a good sport about it and let me publish it as is …

To *Francesca*, my wife, who always encouraged me to write and has gone over everything I've ever written with a fine-tooth comb …

To *Vera*, my mother, who gave me the idea to write this book in the first place when she said, "Keep a journal of your experiences in Florida, dear …"

The Tennis Bubble

CHAPTER 1:

Hope Reigns Supreme

I can still remember five years ago as if it were yesterday. It was Christmas 2006, and we had come back to Paris from Florida for three weeks. Our daughter, Alessandra (Ali), was playing two indoor tournaments, and she was playing out of her mind.

Or rather, she was playing very much in her mind, and that was the beauty of it.

For two weeks, Ali—who had just turned fourteen—decided that she would be the player she was being groomed to be at the Nick Bollettieri Tennis Academy[1], also known as IMG[2]. For two weeks, Ali played every point in every match in the same concentrated way. There were no histrionics, no throwing of racquets, no giving up while ahead, and no meltdowns in the third set. With sometimes two matches a day for two weeks, Ali was able to switch from the hard surface of Nanterre to the soft red clay at the Paris Jean Bouin stadium (where the Lagardère group is located) and wreak devastating victories on her underwhelming opponents. It wasn't that they weren't good but that Ali made them look bad, inconsistent, and weak – just like she had been herself when playing them before.

Before we had gone to Florida, that is.

[1] I often refer to the Nick Bollettieri Tennis Academy as "*NBTA, The Academy* or just *Bollettieri*" in this book.

[2] IMG, the top sports agency in the world at the time, had bought out the Chris Evert and Nick Bollettieri names, putting the Evert Academy on the East wanted to know if East and West were still capitalized (in another book, Mark Mathes told me they weren't. In Canada, we always capitalized them (like in the UK) coast of Florida (in Boca Raton) and the Bollettieri Academy on the West coast (Bradenton).

Before I had decided to move back to the States on a part-time basis for—let's tell it like it is—Ali's tennis.

During those two weeks in 2006, I witnessed a talented but immature girl—with a clear history of tanking, complaining, and throwing matches—suddenly transformed into the exciting, consistent left-handed player I knew she was destined to be. My friend, Bud S, who had been staying with us for a few days at Christmas, said to me after the two tournaments: I guess it's time for you to ease the reins, sit back and enjoy the ride. She's on her own now, and all you have to do is relax and enjoy it!

This is her story and that of the many tennis families who make the annual trek from wherever in the world they stem from to the Nick Bollettieri Tennis Academy in Bradenton, Florida.

This is not the story of an already known quantity—a Roger Federer, Pete Sampras, Bjorn Borg, or Andre Agassi. This is the story of an ordinary budding tennis hopeful and her very supportive family who has constantly assigned too much importance to tennis. This is the story of an adolescent girl with all the tools to become a first-class professional tennis player. This is the story of devastating serves, rifle-crack forehands, pin-point passing shots, and Andre Agassi–like angles that pull the opponent right off the court—of serenity and courage in the face of cheating and frustration. In brief, this is a typical story for all you hopefuls out there—both players and their families—and offers a glimpse of what it takes from all concerned to try and build a champion.

The Tennis Bubble

The Tennis Bubble

CHAPTER 2:

Empty Slate

When a child[3] is first born, it is a empty slate. Its parents haven't put their stamp on it. Neither has life. It is still an "it." "It," in the good sense of the term. It can do anything, be anybody—the president, a famous actor, a rocket scientist, brain surgeon, a tax accountant—the possibilities are endless. It is cute and loving. It smells good and makes you feel wonderful.

It is full of hope, an untouched meadow.

The famous American adage "Name It and Claim It" applies to "it," this as yet unencumbered virgin field. You can name it anything, and it will be that. You can claim it will travel to the moon, and it will do as you say. It is totally virtual, so are your dreams, and it is the vehicle that will fuel your limitless imagination. It is your Id, your Mega-Ego. From the name you've bestowed on it to the tiny clothes you've chosen for it, it is yours and yours for all to see—*yours* as in YOU, you when you were a baby, when you were "it," "you" in the colors it wears now and the ones you probably wore then—or at least one of you might have.

---

[3] I have mostly used the pronouns "he" and "him" to refer *in general* to children or people even though I spend most of the book talking about my daughter. In addition to "you," I sometimes even use "she" and "her" when I'm speaking generally. However, I see no obligation to employ a female pronoun to speak about *mankind,* a neutral word used for hundreds of years to refer to both men and women. I eschew the politically correct terms "womankind" or "humankind," priggish words brought into the English language by do-gooders and fops desirous of selling their sexist agenda or intent on wanting us all to languish in tepid and insipid egalitarianism.

However, as you stand round admiringly, cooing and preening, you are abruptly brought down to earth as your dear *friend* suddenly pipes up out of nowhere: "She's so cute, and you haven't even had time to wreck her yet."

So, the question is, who are you to wreck anything, and why should you? Weren't you just as cute and sweet when you were a few days old? Weren't you full of promise, someone who was perfect?

Well, I don't know how my mate was, nor do I remember how I was at the same age, but I do know that after the first few weeks—after my caring mother-in-law left and went back to Sardinia—we were the only ones around to nurture our daughter, let alone "wreck" her. This is, therefore, the story of how we nurtured and wrecked our daughter in the course of parental duty. It is also the story of unfailing parental love in the pursuit of our daughter's development.

My Tennis Background

I first became involved in tennis in Riverdale in the North Bronx. We had just left Montreal at the time because my father had been transferred back to New York. He was a good club player with a terrific forehand. He would later say of me that although I became a better player than he was, I didn't enjoy it as much as he did. Later on, I said the same thing about my daughter, who had also become a much better player than I was.

I was first taught the forehand while my future wife was being born—April 1958—when I was eight years old. At the time, the teaching method was as easy as 1-2-3:

The Tennis Bubble

1. Racquet back
2. Step forward
3. Swing straight out towards the target

As for the backhand, it was always hit flat or sliced—never topped—and you only learned once you got your forehand down right.

Our wood racquets were heavy.

The serve was both hands down, both hands up in a continuous loop, but I learned that later and really didn't have a decent serve until I was twelve. I became a good "A" player—5.0 USTA and 15/2[4] French ranking—later when I moved to France at age 44. I played college tennis for half a year at the University of California, Berkeley. I continued to play local tournament tennis until I was fifty when, from one day to the next, I couldn't play properly anymore—my head no longer moved independently from my torso when I turned to hit on my right side.

And I was a right-handed player.

---

[4] The French have a complicated way of ranking tennis players but it is much more accurate than its American equivalent in that one knows the ability of a player just by his ranking, provided the player has been playing continuously and competitively for a few months at least:

Players start off non-ranked in the bottom of the fourth division (bottom of the pyramid) and move up through the divisions to the first division (top of the pyramid). Some eventually make it up to the "promo" (promotion) or top national ranking and then they are numbered 1-50. (Top French pros like Gael Monfils or Jo-Wilfried Tsonga would be in the top five players, for example.)

The origin of ranking categories like "30/4, 15/2, or 2/6" stems from the handicap system: A player who is better than another might "give" 2 points (30) for four games to another, or in the case of 15/2, he might "grant" 1 point (15) for two sets to another. Today, handicaps are not observed but the ranking system remains: the lower the ranking number a player has in France, the stronger he is.

I suspected my "head or neck problem" was due to extensive work done on "improving my forehand and serve," which I undertook from 1998 to 2000 when I was between the ages of 48 – 50, but I could never prove this. I believe the tennis teacher I had at the time was responsible for my tennis demise, but again, I could never prove this.

Basically, therefore, I lost my own tennis when Ali was eight years old, and as a result, I could no longer serve as a reliable instructor/tennis role model for her, even though I wanted to.

As for my father, he had left France as a young man, was the oldest in his family and apparently the most intelligent—so it was believed—and was a good chess and tennis player. When I was four and five, he taught me chess, and although I played, I was not interested enough to become an accomplished chess player and compete in tournaments.

I came to understand that competition is what distinguishes the good from the excellent and is really the only way to go once one has achieved a certain level of play.

Whatever the sport. Whatever the activity.

Real competitors want to measure their particular level of excellence against that of others of the same level. Non-competitors are content to just play well at whatever level they happened to attain.

My father was the latter type of guy.

In tennis, that is.

As for me, I imagined myself to be the former type of guy—a true competitor—but something was missing, something that I needed to ingest to get to the next level. That something was confidence. I can't remember all the matches I lost while ahead, not even way ahead, like 6-0, 5-0, 30-15. I won't go into why except to say that I had been traumatized as a kid by several primarily sports-related incidents. I remember that my main concern for Ali was that she NOT be traumatized by anything in the way I had been traumatized.

Even so, in bringing up Ali, I believed in the dictum: expect nothing, no excuses, do something (and in that order) as enumerated by an old friend of our family, Al B, who died in 2007. The thing that bothered me most was that she expected a lot, gave a lot of excuses, and didn't always do something but in all fairness, didn't I do the same thing growing up? I tried not to think so, but I'm sure I did.

In fact, in analyzing the great competitors, they often expect nothing, give no excuses, and do a lot. Naturally, this is only one extreme, but—day in, day out—the best competitors are close to this extreme.

Tennis is War

But it's a *fun* war, although not for everyone.

If we didn't have competitive games, we might all be killing each other. With tennis, we enter into an absurd world where the object is to hit the ball within a rectangle where the other guy is not. The harder we make it for the other guy, the better we become and the more fun the two of us should have. Forget cooperation. Conflict is the way to go.

Incident One

Consider this:

I played a challenge ladder match once with a guy I'd never met before he came to my place to play. (I lived in Los Angeles in a condo complex with its own tennis court.) He looked a little bit like the now-dead Oklahoma bomber Timothy McVeigh—now that I think about it—but this was 1990, not 1995. He had a solemn expression on his face, and other than, "Richard, I'm here to play our challenge match," said absolutely nothing.

We walked down to the courts in silence and played the first set. He continued his silence as I made all the calls, called out the score—both when serving and returning—and won 6-0. He took his Wilson profile racquet and, suddenly belting out a primal scream, shattered it on the net post. Then he became very serious and calm.

We played the second set, and there was the same result. He took his second Wilson profile—about $200 in those days, a considerable price—and destroyed it as well. Then he shook my hand cordially and left without a word.

Incident Two

I played a notorious cheater in Los Angeles once who qualified his two-inch hook—that is, my ball was two inches *in,* but he called it out anyway—as only one-quarter of an inch *out*!

I guess he wanted to make me feel better.

This man's son was also a player and had been so ingrained with cheating—by his father, obviously—that he even took a gun to an opponent who had dared describe one of his cheating calls a cheat.

Incident Three

I had been assigned to "help" referee a junior match for eleven-year-olds in my local French club in the early 2000s. Two boys were in the middle of the third set. The boy returning serve was constantly sniveling and not giving his all, as well as crying every time he made a bad shot. His father was on the sidelines on his side and aggressively watching his match—that is, he was making threatening gestures at his son between every point. Twice I warned the father to stay out of the match, but he couldn't help intervening.

Finally, he couldn't take it anymore and called the boy over to the sidelines—the boy was very reluctant to go to him—and when he got there, the man grabbed him and punched him in the face. Naturally, I went over to confront the father, but he waved me off, saying it was "good" for his son to get punched when he cried and that he could do what he wanted with his own son. I told him he could but not with me in the chair, and I walked off and canceled the match.

How it used to be

When we were in high school, we used to buy fake plastic racquets for young children, go out in the rain—it didn't rain much in California in those days, but when it did, it was a big event—and play hard with them until they broke.

Those days were fun. Why am I telling you these things?

Kids don't seem to have the same fun on the court today except at Halloween when they all dress up and play in costume. But that's organized craziness which is not as much fun.

What it's like to be a tennis parent

The short answer is that it's not easy. And despite what some people think, it is also not necessarily "natural" for a child to become a tennis player.

What is natural is that a child wants to emulate his parents, friends, and others and do what they do. It is enjoyable and natural to hit the ball and keep it going over the net. It is learned behavior to complete the "tennis player" profile by learning how to score and advanced learned behavior to want to win.

At first, a child wants to win because he wants our approval, and we want him to win so we can say he's exceptional, even "better than others." This is because we have our own egos to feed, even though we don't like to admit it.

The problem is when "winning" is confused with "being better than others."

Our parental ego is interwoven with a child's natural desire to please. Paradoxically, a child will really only get better if he focuses on and *enjoys* hitting the ball correctly, not "winning," so to speak, against any old opponent. However, as a child grows and improves, "winning" does have its place in further motivating the child to "play someone new" or "play again." The more you win, the more you play, the more adulation you receive, and the better you get. Winning is important and, let us not forget, winning a match is not only the object of the game. It's also the first step towards enjoying competitive tennis.

The will to win ... *or* ... how do we transform a "normal" child into a Tennis Champion?

I must admit that I did have an agenda when our daughter was first born: I wanted her to become a great tennis player, and even a professional one, *if she was good enough and had the desire to be one.*

I brought her to the tennis courts in her pram so she could hear the sounds of tennis balls going back and forth. When she became a toddler, I observed her closely to see if she was left-handed because left-handedness was an advantage on the court[5].

---

[5] Aside from Alessandra, the three of us in the family are right-handed and left-lateralized. Ali is the other way: left-handed and right lateralized. Most of us have one dominant right or left hand and foot. However, lateralization refers to what side one prefers using while doing many different tasks that don't necessarily require a dominant hand or foot, e.g., picking things out of a car, riding a scooter, sweeping the floor, buttoning one's shirt, etc.

Being left-handed was only an advantage if one learned to exploit the court's geometry, especially on the ad side. I thought: she had a good arm, she was left-handed—why shouldn't she become a "champion?"

Instead of someone else?

Why should I leave it to other parents to "develop my child" when I was more than capable, even though I hadn't proved myself as a world-class competitor?

And other thoughts came to mind:

Why is it important to progress in tennis?

How much do you know about what you want to be while you're growing up?

In other words, how much do you really know what you want before others talk you into it and shove their own ideas down your throat, i.e., if you are highly impressionable, and most young people are, at least for a while?

Don't we all absorb snippets of feeling and decision-making by watching others and seeing how they work things out?

What keeps us going and keeps our dream for our children alive?

Why is it important to progress QUICKLY in tennis?

I think progression is the natural order of things. Use your talent or lose it and nine times out of ten, the kids who stagnate or regress regularly give up the game more quickly than the others.

Why do anything if there is no goal?

There is a natural order of things in tennis: First, you learn strokes and technique, then tactics, and finally, you learn how to play competitive tennis and put it all together and climb the ladder. What is more complicated than that? When people say they don't want to play competitive tennis—as if "normal" tennis were standing in place just hitting balls to each other over the net—is that exercise more normal than running the other guy all over the court and trying to trap him into losing? One guy's loss is the other guy's win, and most of the time, the guy who loses will usually give credit to the guy who beat him because that is the nature of sport in general, and tennis in particular.

What's wrong with this scenario?

Why use tennis for exercise alone? Is brute exercise fun? Besides keeping you fit, competitive tennis is a fun game involving strenuous exercise, pitting your will and wits against another.

Why not just let kids do what they want to do? Choice?!

Many parents pretend to give their kids choices, but they actually choose the path of least resistance, so the parent gets to do what he really wants to do.

Does the kid have a choice?

Am I really putting the kid in front of the computer, TV, game player, etc., and letting the kid decide, letting him be whatever he wants to be?

Or am I borrowing a few hours of quiet time?

If I say to the kid that she should read books, but I don't, will the kid choose to read? If I tell the kid to play his musical instrument, but I don't, will the kid play willingly?

Probably not. Sounds good, but I think this is just laziness on the part of the parents.

Everyone has an idea of what one wants from one's offspring. It's hypocritical to say one doesn't. So why not try to mold the kid into what one wants right from the start—if, and this is a big if—the glove fits? Most of the time, the glove does not fit, but what's the harm in trying at first? Then, of course, the parent should have the humility to realize that he is right or wrong and to orient the kid accordingly.

If you don't give the kid "your" choices at first, won't his first choices turn into "following" the other sheep round at school?

When Little Johnny at school has an iPad, isn't my giving my kid one so he can be like Johnny not a choice but a way of buying down time for myself? In other words, is it to stop the screaming? The luxury of choice should be given to those who've experienced life a little and learned the consequences of choice, i.e., *not* young children. If a child is given nothing to like or hate, what alternative can that child have in the future?

What I'm saying is that kids' choices are formed right from the outset by us. When Andre Agassi's father tries to hypnotize his infant son by moving a tennis ball in front of his eyes while he is in his crib, the father's choosing *for* his son before he has a say in it. When I realize our daughter is a lefty and give her balloons to hit with her left hand, am I trying to prepare her for a professional tennis career?

Of course, I am.

Does she have a choice? I guess she could choose not to hit the balloons. If I keep her in a stroller beside the court while I play my match, she automatically registers the sounds and rhythm of tennis—this is experience, not choice. And does my daughter really have a choice when I nag to my wife—a few years later down the line now—about my daughter, who has been watching TV non-stop for a couple of hours?

"She just doesn't want to pl-a-a-a-yyy."

And then I add sarcastically, saying it directly to my daughter in question:

"Oh, I see we want to watch more television, yes?"

"But you bought the Sky TV for me, Dad!"

"Yes, but I didn't think that was all you wanted to do."

She has made a choice, i.e., watch TV rather than play tennis, but I won't accept this alternative. Because I know that if she practices hard now, she'll be in a much better position later. What will I say to her later IF she says, "*I could have been a contender,* but you didn't push me hard enough—on my volley, my movement, my doubles skills, my composure on the court ..." The list goes on. By being pro-active rather than reactive, I anticipate her future criticisms, and I won't have anything to reproach myself for. However, the things I *will* be criticized for are not being tough enough on her and letting her do whatever she wants.

When I was a kid, everything revolved around sports and school. I wanted my daughter to grow up in this same way. Thus, when I bought a Sky transmitter and English Sky service from England to France so that she would always have English and French, my thinking was that I was preparing my daughter's English and future life in places other than France. The hidden expectation was that she would be reasonable and watch just a certain amount of TV.

Was this a sensible assumption to make about an eight-year-old child?

Didn't I always really want her to choose tennis over television?

And behind this thinking—especially since I was always available—wasn't I was just angry about being available 24/7 and constantly taken for granted? Wasn't I furious about never being appreciated or listened to enough?

In my defense, I was very one-track about our daughter, and had it not been for my insistence that everything be based on either studies or sport (tennis) or physical training related to tennis, I doubt she would have become as good as she did. In fact, as a father, I was fortunate to have always been available, even if it only meant seeing to Ali's homework or sports activities.

The fact remained that, had I not been there, Ali probably would never have started tennis.

When I do something, I like to do it right, and it bothers me if a job is done halfway. She might have started something else, and maybe she would have been more successful at it. But she probably wouldn't have become as good a tennis player.

And so, I return to how good Daughter Alex could have become had we just let her stay in regular school in France and not moved to the U.S.? Would she have enjoyed the sport more or less? As a family, we attended two tennis camps at the Nick Bollettieri Tennis Academy in 2003-4. As a family, we decided to move back to the U.S.in the fall of 2005, so Ali could focus on tennis and studies during her high school years. Would she have quit the game if we hadn't moved? Probably not, but would she have been as good?

Our Choice at first, the Kid's Choice later

By 2005—Ali's 13th year—we realized that it was time to transform thought into action. We *thought* she wanted to become a tennis champion—at least from what she told us at the time. The next four years would be crucial in deciding whether Ali was to 1) become a professional or 2) a good college player. Choice 2 implied using her tennis to get a full-time scholarship in a four-year university of her choice.

Up until this time, we had often been discouraged with Ali's tennis. We tried to be very objective about her, but then she would play a great match or have a good tournament which would have us genuinely believe she could be a top player. Unfortunately, much of the time, she didn't play as well as she could.

I return to what I said in the beginning: This book is about the parents and their child-athlete. It is about the child's will to win and everything that helps or interferes with it. During an adolescent's life, strong emotions come into play. If these are correctly harnessed, then the desire to win is increased. If not, then the desire goes away.

In everything I have undertaken personally, my feeling has always been: Why not me, why someone else?

I am not a watcher, so why should my kids be?

I have tried to transfer that feeling to those close to me—to my wife and kids: be an active doer, not a watcher. From a parental standpoint, this book primarily reflects my point of view. A kid's perspective can be different and probably is, even though he's really in our clutches before the age of puberty.

However, all three points of view—the child's and that of each parent—point either to a tennis result or the lack of one. Thus, this book's interest will not be how our goal in building a tennis champion is realized. There have been plenty of books like that. Our interest is in describing a more typical experience: that of the everyday family attempting to promote a talented youngster. The appeal here is how we tried to do everything "right" or "by the book," so to speak—how we sacrificed and where we came up short or where we succeeded, depending on how you look at it— and our advice to other parents who have the same idea.

In business terms, when is more less, and when is less more?

It's important to me to be able to justify the fact that if I were to die tomorrow, I would have done everything I could have done at the time (I was always pro- rather than re- active from 2002-2010), the time of Ali's formative tennis years). And that's why I have written this book.

The Tennis Bubble

The Tennis Bubble

CHAPTER 3:

Tennis Life in France

I forgot to say that I'm an American raised in Canada and California with a native Italian but American-naturalized wife and an Italo-American young son and teenage daughter.

I also happen to live most of the time in France now.

I have made tennis a priority in my life and have tried to bestow this philosophy on my family. I have a ball machine, racquets, balls, tennis court, stringer, practice wall but above all, I have the time and interest to devote to any one of our family members besotted by the game …

… So, when Alessandra was about due in November 1992, in Santa Monica, California, it was only natural that I happened to be on a tennis court—apparently, my father had been playing, too, when I was born—and sitting down during a changeover next to my good friend and opponent that day, Steve K, I glanced at my beeper to see that my wife had called. She was starting to have contractions, so I concluded I'd better get home pronto to make myself useful should we have to run to the hospital. It turned out that Thursday night, the twelfth of November, these contractions were only a harbinger of things to come. Two days later, on Saturday morning, November 14th, Alessandra was born.

Fifteen months and many tennis matches, mudslides, riots, droughts, floods, and earthquakes later—including the big Northridge earthquake of January 1994—we left Southern California for France, where I had relatives.

We called our daughter Alessandra, but later on, it was she who insisted on being called "A-le"—"Ahh-lay"—two syllables—since that is how Italians shorten Alessandra.

I stuck with *Ali*.

Ali was brought up in France in French and British schools, spoke English and Italian at home, and thus grew up with three native languages: English, French and Italian.

Saint-Germain-en-Laye

When we first moved to France, we settled in Saint-Germain-en-Laye, a thousand-year-old French town perched atop a hill and which happened to be the birthplace of Sun King Louis XIV.[6] We lived on Rue des Ursulines, and across from our house was a large, grassy courtyard in an apartment complex where I would toss balls to her and teach her how to ride a bike. She was three at the time, and we would take our books or mini-racquets and play. By age four, she was able to put racquet to ball but not very well.

---

[6]Louis XIV was born in 1638 in a large chateau that was first built by Louis VI in 1122 and had served Kings and Queens ever since. Later on, after Louis XIV had removed to Versailles, he would continue to return to his birthplace and 'country cottage' chateau where he would start his hunts down into the Valley of the Seine and across the forest of Le Vésinet (where we moved three and a half centuries later in 1998).

Le Vésinet

By age five, we had moved to the next town over, Le Vésinet, where we had Ali taking extra tennis classes and group lessons. I was good friends and teammates with Didier E and Olivier F, our local club pros. Ali was in one of Didier's classes with three other boys, two of whom were very talented and consistent players, and Ali improved significantly during her time in this class. Ali also took private lessons with serve and volleyer Olivier F.

There were also holiday *stages* or training camps when school was not in session. I enrolled Ali in all of these training camps, where she continued to improve. She would often play with the same boys she was in regular tennis class with and started to do minor club and inter-club tournaments where she would take out the opposition. It was fabulous to watch her improve from one day to the next.

Then political problems within our club arose. The club had been losing members and money the previous years, debts were accumulating, and people were taking advantage of lax club rules. The prestige of the club was suffering. Concerned about seeing things change, one tennis parent of a talented boy player came to me to ask if I would be interested in running the club.

I wasn't, nor did I want to make time to do so.

So, he took it over himself, made himself President, and took on another tennis parent as Vice President. Unfortunately, neither knew how to run a tennis club. Nevertheless, both these men had promising juniors who were older than Ali, and they wanted to push their kids ahead. To do this, they hired another big-name pro who was to become the personal coach of both the son and the other man's daughter.

Then heads began to fall under the reign of these two dads. Gone were my friends Serafin, Didier, and Virgil, the new coach who had been hired especially for the new directors' "rising stars." A new wave "Zen" coach was hired who spent his time watching people play and saying nothing. Apparently, he felt "words of criticism/advice" could affect the student's inner ability to play and control himself. Then he left (or was pressured out, I never knew), and three girls who were role models to my daughter left. We contemplated leaving ourselves but didn't.

This was a mistake—it was 2001—but as I had some free time to work with Ali on the side, we left her in her program, even though it was not in the best interests of her tennis. Fortunately, I was able to play with her after school and sometimes during lunch to make up for her weak class. Then one of us would take the busy girl to dance, but she neither had the time nor interest to keep this up and dropped ballet.

Ditto for her piano and guitar lessons.

I noticed she didn't drop her tennis, however. She never missed practice, seemed pretty cool during matches, and sometimes asked me to play. As a girl, she was very pretty and feminine, but she had big strong hands, a great touch, and was a powerful lefty tennis player. Every year, we would watch some of her (and my!) favorite players like Nathalie Tauziat, Patty Schnyder, upcoming Amelie Mauresmo, and Anna Kournikova at the Gaz de France indoor Paris tournament at the Stade de Coubertin.

However, on a less positive note, she had average speed, was a little distracted, and not "athletic" enough. She also didn't listen to or show enough respect for her tennis teachers and teachers in general, and I think this was—in retrospect—due to the difficulty she had in concentrating. Generally, and in everything.

Outside of tennis, she demonstrated little desire to play concentration games like chess, Scrabble, or even games in general, but she was energetic and social and had many friends at school.

During this time, Ali went from being unranked to 30/3—a three-spot jump at the time—in the French ranking system.

Thus, when Ali was eight, we became a real tennis family—one that lives, sleeps, breathes, and eats tennis. That is, in 2001, we started "changing" our lives for tennis. First of all, we stopped our annual skiing trip to the French Alps so that Ali wouldn't get hurt skiing.

Every school holiday[7] there was a tennis tournament. Birthday invitations were often turned down so Ali would be ready for—not sick for, not tired for, but rather up for— a tennis tournament.

Family get-togethers and other non-tennis, non-essential social events were eschewed, ignored, or delayed. Often this was because they occurred during tennis tournaments or prize-giving ceremonies, which was most of the time.

The year before, in 2000, there had been tryouts for "La Ligue," the high-powered tennis league of our "province" or "department" in France. We lived in the "Yvelines" province, just west of Paris, a province comprised of important cities such as Rambouillet and Versailles. These try-outs were for kids born in 1992 who would turn eight years old during 2000.

---

[7] In France, every eight weeks of classes is followed by two weeks of school holiday.

Ali made the first three cuts of these try-outs and was part of the final group of ten they *might* set up for special training—at first, three hours a week, then three hours a day as the child got older and into secondary school. This was the essence of the "sports-study" afternoon program that would follow intensive French school in the morning. It was a huge deal to be taken into this elite group, and we were hoping she would be accepted.

She wasn't.

They only accepted five of these final ten girls, and Ali was number six or seven. I never knew. The unofficial but verifiable report on her was that—compared to the other "élite girls"—she was "technically good, but not in shape, physically slow and weak, and didn't have a great competitive attitude."

Whatever!

The Ligue's philosophy was that a child must have the fundamentals—the drive and physical desire to grind out points early—and they, the Ligue, would teach them the tennis techniques. Whether a child knew how to play at eight was immaterial to them in 2000. It was essential that a child have the drive and means to play, be teachable, and that the Ligue take over as trainers.

This assessment immensely angered me since this same Ligue the following year took on a friend of Ali's who hardly knew how to play. However, this friend was physically taller, very eager and strong, and exhibited a desire to play. But she could barely hit a ball over the net.

However, she had a very aggressive mother.

In other words, a mum who yaps trumps a father who watches and listens. We have to remember we are in France, where the *spoken word* often overrides everything else, especially can-do action and know-how.

The contrast for me was too obvious to miss, and I vowed that I would compensate for this injustice and always give Ali the best instruction possible because I believed in her, in her technique. And she was much faster than they claimed. However, I wanted her tennis ability to speak for itself and stand out on its own. It seemed to me in France at the time that a child need only be eager and strong and have parents who had the time and the character to be very aggressive in their promotion of said child, and that was the ticket for admission.

I was neither that type of parent, and neither was I a salesman. But I knew something about tennis, and I had time for her.

In 2000, I was still an eager, competitive senior club player, and I began to play tennis with her more and more. She started to win tournaments at her age level and above, but she'd always come up against these "Ligue" girls who would beat her easily.

It seemed as if she had a complex against them since she hadn't been admitted to their elite group and often played worse than she usually would. I was forced to acknowledge *at the time* that the Ligue was right about Ali, but I knew in my heart that she was, and would become, a much better player than what she gave out.

As I mentioned before, 2000 was also the year that certain unrefined elements took over our club. One of our top pros, Didier, was forced out and transferred to the Riviera at Cagnes-sur-Mer, where he raised three excellent boy players. The eldest, Jonathan, is now in the top 400 ATP and was the number1 ITF junior player in 2006.

Le Vésinet, 2001-2002

As I mentioned before, Ali was eight and turning nine at the time and—due to no fault of her own—was improving slowly tennis-wise. She was paired with slightly older girls for team matches, and aside from the odd tournament together, there was not much chemistry in their relationship. There was no fierce competition between them, nor was there the desire or the spark to push each other higher and higher up the tennis ladder.

Ali no longer played with the good boy players in our club and was kept away from one other girl player one year older than she because her parents thought their darling was "too good" to play with Ali. This "too good to fail" player ended up leaving the game early on.

Outside the classes and team matches she attended, I had Ali take more private lessons with different pros who came and went from the club that year—after all, I had a court in my garden—and they all thought she had potential.

I forgot to say that when she was seven—I was always looking for signs that my daughter had the potential to go the professional route—one pro told me it was just up to me: What did I want to do with here? If I wanted, I could have her turn professional when she was twelve. But I would have to steer her in the right direction, which would mean having too much of a say in her development and her missing time from English school in the International French Lycée system.[8] Other than the English instruction, she went to a regular primary school in French like everyone else.

Chatou 2002-2005

After watching Alex waste her 2001-2 year in Le Vésinet, my wife persuaded me to send her to nearby Chatou and train with Emmanuel Planque.[9] Planque saw a lot of potential in her lefty cross-court shot and excellent serve, but stressed the need for her to train physically. He also had trouble getting his head around the fact that she could play really well one day and quite poorly the next. This was not *"cohérent,"* he muttered, in his very French way.

---

[8] At the time, she attended school four days a week like other French children except one morning and afternoon per week (one day total) were exclusively set aside for British instruction for native English speakers.

[9] Michael Llodra's and Fabrice Santoro's former coach and (last I heard) the coach of up-and-coming French stars, Guillaume Rufin, Axel Michon and (much later on) Luca Pouille.

From 2002-2005 (ages 9-12), Ali played for Chatou in their accelerated competition program. Nine and a half years old in 2002, she was paired with a couple of eleven-year-old girls on the under 11 team. She also trained with some of the better boy players, and unlike Le Vésinet, Chatou was a much younger, competition-oriented club. In addition, Chatou coached trained big-name players. Former top tenner Hicham Arazi and Michael Llodra had been trained there as well as top French junior Alice Bélichat, "big time," or "*haut niveau*," players.

After three years at Chatou, Ali went from 30/3 to 15/4, then to 15/2, a total jump of seven French ranking levels.

Her progress was not just due to her commitment to her new club. We, as her parents, also made sure that Ali was given proper hitting partners and signed up for every tournament she could possibly play. In addition, I played a lot with her, and she also took lessons with outside coaches, Olivier F and Florence S.

Bollettieri First Visit

My wife and I were still not satisfied with her progress in France and decided to visit the Bollettieri Tennis Academy in October 2003 during the French school Halloween holiday in late October. It would be a good break for us—after having spent almost eleven continuous years in France—and we would be able to participate in the Bollettieri adult program as well. As for the little one,[10] he would hang out with his nanny, a French woman whom he adored, as well as soak up the sounds of bouncing tennis balls.

We did everything by internet and booked the entire ten days of the Halloween holiday. We traveled as a family—plus nanny—from Paris to Miami and stayed with my friend, Bud S, in Port St. Lucie the first night. We arrived at the IMG Evert Academy the next day (International Management Group), where Ali played a full day of tennis with some solid players and a few pros. The reports on Ali's play were highly favorable and encouraging. It was such a difference from France, where people were much less enthusiastic and much more critical.

---

[10] Max(imilian) Bonte was born in May 2002.

The next day was spent at the Rick Macci—pronounced "Macy" and not "Matchy" as it would be in Italy—Tennis Academy just north of Miami. Rick was another legendary coach known for grooming very young players, often as young as four. Rick's operation was held in a public park just behind some hotel or resort community, and I was impressed by his youngsters' quality of play. They looked very fit and were supervised closely by Rick and some of his assistants. However, Rick was not interested in our daughter. He didn't comment on her—even though we asked him—but rather on the "movement" of another one of his own students. In other words, his silence on Ali was tantamount to an unfavorable comparison to another girl. At least we knew where we stood with him.

The same afternoon, we made our way up to Orlando for Disneyland and dolphin watching.

After eleven years out of the country, I was impressed by the organization and professionalism of everybody and everything American: from the way my fellow citizens served pancakes and calorie-packed breakfasts at Denny's to the mechanical yet enthusiastic way they ran tennis camps.

After a couple of wonderful days in the different theme parks and slowly making our way up to Bollettieri, we arrived for our weeklong adult program for us and a short-timer program for our daughter. The place was known as the "Toughest Playground in the World," and after three days of tennis—8 a.m. until 4:30 p.m., mind you—we adults were due for massage therapy which we underwent for the next three days just to be able to survive the physical workout. Our daughter was in better shape than we were but still found it challenging. She even had a private lesson with Nick at $500 an hour.[11]

When our daughter told Nick, "I know, I know" how to do a certain stroke that he was explaining, Nick shot out to the others watching: "What is she, French?!" and then responded directly to her. "Young Lady, over here I do the talking, and you do the listening, capisc'?" I appreciated Nick's frankness at the time and came to like Nick a lot in the many discussions I had with him over the next few years. After a week at Bollettieri, we were impressed enough to return during Christmas a year later.

Before going back to France, however, we were approached by Chip Brooks,[12] veteran leader of the Bollettieri adult program but someone who had been with the Academy since day one. Chip was impressed enough with our daughter to get us involved in a Distance Learning Program with Bollettieri assistant coach and ball feeder Greg Hill. Distance Learning involved sending tapes of our child playing tennis in France to Greg and Nick in Florida for a monthly fee of $700.[13]

---

[11] Since then, his hourly rate doubled in less than five years and now I don't know what it is.

[12] Chip was top-tenner Jelena Jankovic's coach throughout 2010.

[13] During these boom times (2003-4), the numbers were always getting higher and it was common knowledge that the Bollettieri Academy just wanted your

This system only partially worked because the videos we made were not the best, even though Nick's comments were quite good on the tapes they sent back in return. However, from our perspective, the videos kept Ali in Nick's eye and prepared our return to Bollettieri during Christmas, 2004.

During these holidays, she worked with Lance L and his crew on strategy and tactics. She took another two lessons with Nick at $500 per hour, and we decided to come to Florida for at least three years so that our daughter could have the opportunity of becoming a "contender."

Naturally, this whole business was going to cost us a lot. It had already cost us a lot. The two weeks at IMG-Bollettieri, the two lessons with Nick, the whole trip, etc., but was it worth it?

It was.

When I think back at how she played and how she improved during her stay—even her short visits—I realize we did the right thing. Our daughter was a lefty, she had started young, and she played with proper technique. Now she needed to put it all together. The only question mark was her mental and physical ability. As well as the biggest question of all: how much did she really want to compete?

---

money.

During the next eight months, there were discussions with lawyers and tax people because what we were going to do was turn into American residents again. We had been French residents for many years, and now that we were to become American domiciled again, there were tax benefits to be gained and a new American way of life to be offered to our kids. That being said, I still didn't want to cut my roots in France, though. Plus, what I really wanted to discover was whether our daughter really "had what it took." My concern was whether Nick and the Bollettieri people were just saying what we wanted to hear or whether they really believed in our daughter. More importantly, I wanted to see how she competed with the best. I wasn't sure at the time whether she was competing with the best.

Or just the richest?

Help on these questions came from an intelligent but overly pessimistic—or so I felt at the time—Frenchman, Monsieur X. Monsieur X had initially run into our French nanny walking around the campus at IMG with Max. (The French always seek each other out. I guess it's the same with all nationalities).

Monsieur X had taken us aside when we first arrived in Florida in 2003 to let us know that "everything was not what it seemed at IMG." There were many things going on that we didn't know about, and that IMG was basically a money-making operation that was second to none.

We learned that it was essential to maintain the status quo and hunky-dory dream-like atmosphere of IMG. And thus, there was much unspoken information that needed to remain so. For example, there were poisonous snakes on campus that people didn't want to talk about. There were deaths from over-training and people—who had been trained by know-nothing trainers and pseudo-coaches—injured for life. There were hidden plumbing and water issues in the villas and all sorts of fishy things going on.

After an hour of talking with Monsieur X, I wondered what I wanted to go to Bollettieri for. Why would anyone want to go to Bollettieri? But then I also wondered about the source of this information—that is, about him—and his family. Why was he still there after three years at the time? I never found the answer.

I thought about what he said, but my mind was focused on tennis—my daughter's tennis—and now back in France during late 2003, I continued to think about our ten days in Florida and started looking forward to our next visit.

Bollettieri 2nd Visit

Thus, when we came back to Bollettieri a year later, in late 2004, we were not only thinking about tennis—we also intended to buy something on campus. We looked at condos and villas with Jeri B (Nick's first wife in charge of villa rentals and sales) and her colleague David L. We also pursued our talks with Monsieur X, attended the adult program, and put our daughter in a two-week short-timer program with Lance L. Lance employed ex-college player, Margie Z who is still there today and works with talented juniors. The two of them ran what was called the Strategy Zone, a program that emphasized "building the point" in tennis: Each winning point can be basically broken down into a series of shots that *control, hurt, and finish off* an opponent.

We liked their concept—"control, hurt, finish." That was the way most tennis points worked anyway. Lance was a statistician and cameraman, very good at filming and studying tennis, and knew the fundamentals of the world's second-toughest game.[14] Apparently, he had never been more than a high school player himself, but he had a sound grasp of the game, and I always found he made sense to me.

---

[14] Someone once told me golf was the toughest. Maybe it is, mentally. I wouldn't know except to say that it doesn't compare—physically—to tennis.

When you think about it, it was clear that one needed to control the point, hurt the opponent with either a sharp-angled, short or deep shot, and then finish him off. This was just a way of verbalizing but easy to remember—"control, hurt, finish." Margie and Lance also used famous Australian movement coach David Bailey's movement tapes and came up with several patterns to use. Their thing was angles, and they thought that Ali had what it took to produce these angles: in their words, she had the best hands of all their students.

Naturally, Monsieur X and his family thought that Lance was just an IMG crony and that he was not to be trusted. X added that no one trusted anybody since everything had changed for the worse at IMG since the organization was only out to steal one's money.

However, we always felt that anything Monsieur X said was actually determined by his son's lack of success in the Academy. Had his son succeeded like Monsieur X thought he might when they first moved to Bollettieri in 2001, then maybe Monsieur X wouldn't have been so bitter towards the Academy.

This was a moot point, however.

It turned out that their son did go on to a four-year university with a half-term scholarship, so he partially succeeded. And these were the ones who did *not* become pros; they were the majority at 96%. A good number of them went on to play semi-professional tennis in one of the many colleges in the U.S. with four-year, all-expenses-paid college "scholarships."

I use the word "scholarship" ironically—maybe a twenty-hour-a-week *part-time job* playing tennis is more to the point—as these kids work their behinds off on the court. They practice just as much as the pros *and* pursue a course of studies as well. In college, one can't play one's sport without maintaining a minimal C average, and many of these players score B and above. I very much admire college student-athletes because they work very hard at both their sport and their studies.

However, there were many differences in parents' expectations of their kids. Some parents knew right from the beginning that their kids were going to play tennis in college. Others were never sure since their kids might/might not be fantastic in their studies or incredible in their sport, so it was unsure what would happen.

This uncertainty fuels the dream:
- Will my son/daughter become a great player?
- Will she become a star?
- In the U.S., everything is possible—so we are taught—so why not us?
- Why should someone else be a star?
- Why do most of us look outside ourselves for others to become stars?
- Alternatively, if you have to worry about being a star, then you're not one. Just do your job and get on with it!

The Tennis Bubble

CHAPTER 4:

Journal: Bollettieri Dreams

Nick Bollettieri IMG Tennis Academy: Bradenton, Florida, 2005-2008

The following is a day-by-day accounting, journal-style,[15] of our three full school years at the Nick Bollettieri Tennis Academy (IMG) in Bradenton, Florida.

On August 20, 2005, we left as a family from Paris to live at the Bollettieri Academy.

Previously, during the early part of 2005, I had bought two villas: A 3-3—3-bedroom, 3-bath—to live in and a 3-2—3 bed, 2-bath—to rent or to use as an office or as a place for friends and family. Since the 3-2 was furnished and the 3-3 wasn't, we moved into the 3-2 for a month before buying furniture for and painting the 3-3. Then, we left the nanny alone in the 3-2 and moved into the 3-3. But we were a little leery of the larger place since the former owner had committed suicide the previous May.[16] This fact, of course, was not disclosed to us—only that he had died—but Monsieur X, to his credit, had called us in France to let us know the truth. He did so to see if we still wanted to move but also to give us a way of working down the purchase price since this fact hadn't been disclosed to us. He had a strong point, but we didn't try to exploit this death for a price reduction.

---

[15] Note that most of these journal notes reflect my point of view **at the time of writing** (2005-8) and have not been "re-spun" to correspond to what I know now (2021).

[16] Apparently, this owner was a big finance guy and had become a loner and—although completely dedicated to his three sons—had accumulated so much debt that he took his own life in our bedroom. When we arrived, there

Naturally, we had come to the Nick Bollettieri Tennis Academy when daughter Alessandra was just twelve so she could realize her tennis dreams. When I say "just twelve," I really mean three months shy of thirteen, which is old for the Academy if you want to be a successful product of their system but more on that later. There were kids as young as two in the tennis programs, although I thought these classes were more babysitting than tennis.

You can't argue with the numbers, though, coming up through the system. As I said before, 96% of these kids go on to college, stop playing or quit, but there is still the 4% who become pros. And for the ones who really make it and become famous— the Agassis, Couriers, Sharapovas, and Monica Seleses—they attract thousands of hangers-on who go on to collect their part of the success pie and bring even more student-athletes to Bollettieri. Naturally, as in all things, when the (tennis) hero's star fades, the hangers-on drift away.

---

was a bullet hole in one of the floor tiles. Some handyman mentioned that a hanging plant in a heavy pot had fallen on this tile but I didn't believe him. The former owner's blue suit was in the closet, and the rest of the apartment was painted a muddy, brown color and reflected African themes.

Attitude

During Bollettieri orientation, the kids were given a good talking to:

"Every minute in every day is basically your choice," said the overly healthy, big-breasted woman in "high-waisted shorts and a tight sports shirt. "You can decide to wake up and go to practice or class—or you can sleep. You can decide to go to bed on time or go on your computer for that little bit of 'My Space'[17] time. Or watch that extra TV program. The next day you will have to pay for it if you're tired and can't study or can't run because your body didn't get enough rest the night before. Sure, you can use drugs or drink alcohol or use bad language, but if you do, you will be kicked out or punished, and hopefully, we won't be having this discussion in this room because if we are, it will mean you were doing something you shouldn't, and you've been found out."

"Attitude, attitude, attitude" was the concept she tried to hammer home. One could do anything with a good attitude and nothing with a bad one. I thought back to my days in an all-boys English military school in Canada where our headmaster had written the same word on the blackboard in bold capital letters and then proceeded to speak for an hour and a half about the importance of having a good attitude.

---

[17] Facebook hadn't reached its zenith yet.

Here at Bollettieri, there were all sorts of counselors giving student-athletes and parents a rundown of the rules: Meal rules, curfew rules, behavior and dress rules, etc. For young people, these rules were essential, and when you think about it, how does one keep a bunch of teenage kids in check?

We settled into the IMG routine—an organized, military method of teaching sports, studies, discipline, and the American way. The idea was to militarize the student-athletes—there were soccer, golf, basketball, baseball, tennis, and as of 2007/8, fishing programs, too—as well as their parents and villa owners. Monsieur X was head of the owners' Condo Association Board, and he and his family helped us get acclimated.

We noticed that most of the parents on site were sometimes a father but more often a mother who lived with her children—student-athletes and their siblings—while the other parent was off working in another state, or South America, or Europe, or somewhere else in the world. In this way, the woman could observe the development of their kid (or spoiled brat) first-hand, whatever the case. In our case, there were two of us present, and the trouble was what to do with our younger child. He didn't seem to be as keen on the game—or was it the fact that, at three years and four months, he was just too young to play and didn't want to put up with the extreme heat?

We began to learn about the coaches who supervised our kids. They were all from South America and very experienced. We learned that they would spend the first two weeks watching the kids play matches and deciding who would be in which group. There were three groups for girls aged eleven to fifteen who played either in the afternoon or morning: Percy M's was the top group, Mauricio H's was the middle group, and Hermann's was the bottom group.

Monsieur X told us that Percy's was the best, but Percy was never really interested in Ali. She cried and cried after not being admitted to his group, and I thought, "Here we go again, I'm going to have to fight just like I did in France to get my daughter into the top group."

The thought occurred to me that maybe she didn't belong in his "top" group, whatever that meant. Perhaps she was not good enough? Even though I was sure she was. But since I had told Percy that my daughter had worked extensively with Guillermo P-R in Sardinia and that I wanted her to have a forehand like his and like Federer's in that the racquet would cut through the air like a rapier—unlike a Nadal or Sharapova follow-through on the same side of the head—Percy possibly believed he was going to have trouble with me in that he would have to deal with a meddlesome dad. Since he was very territorial—and wouldn't want to share the credit with someone else should Ali turn into a top player—he never allowed Ali into his group, nor did he work with her privately.

Percy had been at the Academy for ages, as had Jose L., Daniel "Red" A., and many of the others. Were they all burned out from being in the sun too long and lost their freshness and eagerness for the game? Some parents seemed to think so but weren't those the same parents who hadn't seen their kids rise to the same level of greatness they believed they were "ordained" to attain?

Was I to become one of those parents?

Ali settled in with Mauricio, who I thought was excellent one-on-one but seemed to fade in a group setting and who appeared rather unenthusiastic in his teaching. Mauricio was a former World #80—a very respectable ranking—and in the past had won matches over champions like Patrick Rafter. It was my feeling at the time that Mauricio believed a player could only go so far. But since I didn't really talk to him, and he didn't say much either except to say that "Ali was a very talented player," I let things go along and had faith he would do the best for my daughter.

On the other hand, Percy was very dynamic and had the most concentrated, consistent girls in his group. He told me when we ran into him at Gio's—the local pizza-piano bar where many of us tennis-parents often got together Saturday night—that he had been a lawyer and had been very impressed with Ali. Then again, he never took her into his group, nor did his actions speak louder than his words. Nor did he tell me directly that he didn't really appreciate what I had to say.

I've always believed that technically, there is only so much one can do for a player—a kid either has it or doesn't. If you look at what most coaches have to offer, they pretty much give the same general advice: see the ball early, prepare for it, and hit it way out in front. Extend your non-dominant hand—usually the left—towards the ball on your forehand, go low to high on your groundies, reach up and out on your serve, etc. Most coaches say these same things at one time or another.

Then there are the more technical things like for the smash. "Hit the ball before you have to on the smash as it's coming down fast." Or for the forehand, "Don't just sit back hitting open-stance balls but master the *neutral*—formerly "closed"—stance as well by extending the fingers and arm straight out towards the ball with the non-dominant arm."

However, most of Ali's coaches have said the same thing by and large, not because they don't have anything else to bring to the table but because this is how the game is played. When I watch my own daughter play—and I'm only an amateur coach at the basic level—I immediately know what she's doing right and wrong on a technical level, and I have a good idea how she's going to play. What I don't know is if she's going to maintain a good standard for the whole match, and that is because her psychological character is not fully formed.

There was also Head Honcho Gabe J, the director of player development, who swore at the beginning of each year that all Bollettieri coaches were highly taken with their jobs and enthralled with their students. Of course, his view was in stark contrast to that of Monsieur X, who felt that the coaches were tired and cynical and that IMG just wanted your hard-earned dollar. For example, management would take a twenty percent pound of flesh—for life—from the students it asked to sign with IMG. Even Maria Sharapova, who won the year before at Wimbledon (2004), couldn't pocket all her winnings. She started at nine at Bollettieri and would always have to give them twenty percent of her life-long earnings. This whole idea seemed preposterous to me, but it was just another example of greedy human nature.

I mused about this and also about what one guy—whom I happened to come upon working in a nearby stationery store in Bradenton—once said, "Watch out for contracts with IMG. They own the bottom line, and if they ever promise you anything, they'll expect it all back and more in spades."

But isn't this the way the world worked everywhere? Any business worked that way. At the time, I wrote this comment off in my mind.

Our thoughts before coming here were to find an environment for our daughter where she would get the best instruction, play with the best players and be able to do a proper course of college preparatory instruction in English.

What with the internet and the global nature of education today, she's able to not only do that but more, including studying French through correspondence school direct from France. Sure, she wouldn't have her classmates around her and be in her native "French" environment, but she would be able to study French as well as be in the U.S. Anything is possible with the internet, anything.

My general feeling about studies—and I have spent a lot of time in post-graduate work—is this: Not all people should study in a university of higher learning. Nascent plumbers become emerging plumbers, beauty school graduates become beauticians, and *certain* engineering students become rocket scientists.

Not everyone is created equal, as certain feel-good pundits have us believe. We are not all born equal, nor are all of us destined to become professional tennis players. Some are simply better than others. We don't all have to go to Harvard. Don't we start a tournament with one hundred twenty-eight players and end up with two finalists, only one of which is the eventual winner?

As Hurricane Katrina is devastating New Orleans, we buy two vans, three bicycles, and a number of home furnishing items. We also buy furniture for our unfurnished apartment.

We thought about buying it furnished, but after the guy popped himself in our bedroom and we found out the place had an African—a "dark" theme—we thought, why not go in and whitewash it, put in light wood, and modern light wood furniture? The only good thing was that the villa had white plantation shutters. My visiting sister liked them so much, she went and ordered them for our mother's house in the UK. Forget curtains, long live plantation shutters.

There have been many trips to Sarasota, a minimum of thirty minutes in each direction—to deal with furniture and car issues. The U.S. is not as efficient as when I first remember it, despite the computers, or is it *because* of the computers? We had to wait two and a half months to get our complete furniture set. Why? Because certain parts would come from China via Philadelphia, and they understock in their stores around the country. So what it translates down to is the impression that you can have anything you want, but when you dig a little, you find that most items are not in stock, and you have to wait.

As for computers in 2005, they run everything on the campus as well as in the U.S. Everything is online. People here on campus are very pleasant and are always ready to accommodate and help. This is such a change with Europe where vendors wear a perpetual scowl, earn minimum wage, and consider the customer an annoyance rather than a precious plant to be nurtured.[18]

People have a strange way of talking here—not just on campus—but in the U.S. They have a precise vocabulary with respect to business—and Americans are undoubtedly some of the best business and salespeople in the world—but they don't seem to have any words to explain the emotions they are feeling. People use words such as "awesome, like are you serious? and totally" and other such phatic expressions which say, "I'm with you here in the room listening and being with you." This is such a change from Europe, where people cut you off regularly, talk over you, and are very impatient if you have to search for your words.

---

[18]In all fairness, Europe has become only *slightly* more consumer-friendly than what it used to be.

September 2005

Both Robb & Stuckey and Kanes furniture arrives in drips and drabs. Our days consist of watching tennis, waiting for furniture, setting things up, looking for more things for the villas, and supervising our children.

Jocelyne, our nanny, is getting into a routine with Max. School, sleep, beach. Often, as he did in France, he sleeps too much and doesn't go to bed at night. This is the kind of guy who will only sleep if he's really tired, and it doesn't matter where you happen to be. Aren't all kids like this?

Rosanna

Fran and I keep running into an Italian who I thought at first glance was Eastern European because she's very blond and fair-skinned and who seems slightly serious. However, she's hilarious and engaging once you get to know her. She has become Fran's new friend.

Aurelie

Aurelie is a French player in her first year of working for Lance. A woman in her mid-twenties, she has been assigned to Ali. When Aurelie was a child, she used to play with Amelie Mauresmo.[19] Now she likes to teach and works more with Ali than Lance or Margie.

I contacted Emmanuel P to have Ali play as a French woman, and he had his friend Catherine write a letter for her with the *Fédération Française de Tennis* letterhead. Regarding this business/promotion front, I also received Italian letters of endorsement from the *Federazione Italiana Tennis*. When it came to tennis, I never wanted to leave any stone unturned. And I never wanted Ali to burn her bridges, anywhere.

Lance, Margie, and Aurelie seem pleased with Ali and maintain she is playing very well.

---

[19] In 2005-6, Amelie Mauresmo was a top-ten player in the world.

October 2005

The X family members have become more of a pain in the neck than they're worth. We spend much too much time talking about them with our nanny—how they're so negative about everything and how it would be impossible for anyone to do anything if he were to listen to them.

A French-speaking couple—the husband teaches in the program—also warned us that if Ali were to spend too much time with the X family, it might harm Ali and her aspirations at Bollettieri.

Be careful not to hang out with negative people is the message.

One of the big problems we experienced at Bollettieri was guidance: Was it the Academy tournaments that were important or the local super series, the sectional, national, or ITF tourneys?[20] How were we supposed to proceed besides "trial and error"?

---

[20] **Super Series**: the more highly rated local junior tournaments. **Sectionals**: more highly rated junior tournaments which involve that section of the country where one lives (Southeast Florida, Northeast, etc.). **Nationals**: like the name implies, junior tournaments played at the USTA national level divided up into gender and age categories. **ITF**: International Tennis Federation tournaments which give one ITF junior or ATP (men's) or WTA (women's) points depending on the dollar amount of the ITF, the age of the player and whether that player accepts prize money or not. College players aren't supposed to accept any prize money except that which covers their expenses.

For example, Lance told us, "Have Ali do a couple of locals and see where she fits in," but we didn't want to pull her away from the Academy program to do local tourneys. Fortunately, these took place on weekends—unlike tourneys in France which could last for two weeks if one is low-ranked or a few days if one is highly ranked.

I believe a system should have been put in place at Bollettieri whereby a series of tournaments are set up for the kids, and there are "tournament" coaches assigned whose sole job is to set up tournaments for—as well as accompany, time permitting—these kids. As it stands, in 2005, coaches are out there trying to make as much money as possible, parents are trying to figure where to enroll their kids, and the whole system is too hit or miss, too much up in the air.

We're still trying to figure out which tourneys to put her in. "Which tourneys"[21] have always been a problem for us, but with what we spend at the Academy, I do feel that Bollettieri should have special counselors to advise us and lead us the right way. One could retort: "How many kids have both parents on campus to guide them?" Not many, but then isn't this a question of the blind leading the blind? Why don't we get help from the pros who should know a lot better about what is going on?

Ali is spending more and more time with Aurelie in the Lance/Margie/Aurelie triangle. Aurelie has expressed interest in Accent Reduction[22] as she has a very strong accent in English. I'm trying to trade Accent Reduction lessons with her in exchange for tennis lessons for Ali. However, I don't feel that Aurelie wants to put in the time to do it properly.

---

[21] Whether in France or in Florida...

These are the results of Ali's first Grand Prix at NBTA:

- She lost her first round in the main draw but went to the final of the consolation.
- There she lost 8-1 against Gaia Sanesi, a "cool" Italian who has become one of Ali's friends.

Angela Lopera Tournament

Our nanny has discovered gambling in Tampa on the Indian Reservation—legalized gambling. With only one month to go in the United States—her visa runs out in mid-November—she's discovered a venue in which to carry on her "nanny-by-day, gambler-by-night" life that she led in France. Why we allowed this behavior to continue is still a question I ask myself today, but I saw no problem in it then.

---

[22] Accent Reduction involves "reducing" one's foreign accent in English by rendering it more understandable to the native English speaker's ear—any variety of English.

I have bought a large taupe-colored fisherman's hat that I have equipped with a leather tie to keep it on when gusts of wind shoot across the Bollettieri fields and swamps. I wear it with my usual uniform: baggy canvas shorts, leather sandals, Ray-Ban sunglasses, and a T-shirt or colored sports shirt. I grab my leather horse-racing stick,[23] jump on my Wal-Mart—aka made in China—$79 mountain bike that has accumulated an amazing amount of rust in only two months, and ride to the courts. I remind myself to oil it and raise my bike seat as I glide by the dozens of courts packed with kids smacking tennis balls. I glide by runners and golf carts as I cross over the wooden bridge separating Academy Park and the soccer fields from the main tennis courts behind. Below this bridge is a nasty swamp which I imagine to be infested with all sorts of nasties like water moccasins and alligators, although I have never seen one in this particular swamp. I continue on past tangle weed patches near the Soccer Academy and finally arrive at some green clay tennis courts.

It is 2:30 p.m. Francesca has gone to pick up Max at school, and here I am, perched on the horse-racing stick, watching my darling play tennis. Even in the shade, the heat is horrific, and I watch as the sweat pours down her face after she hits each ball. Fortunately, she is wearing a hat, and I assume she's wearing sun cream on her exposed shoulders and upper arms. Her style is pretty smooth unlike that of some of the girls who are "arming" the ball too much and not using their bodies enough to power their shots.

But I wonder about all the noise I'm hearing?! These *are* clay courts, are they not?

---

[23] A sturdy metal cane with a small leather seat that can be used alternatively as a walking stick or a seat to watch sporting events.

Then I realize each girl is "shrieking" as she hits each ball a la Sharapova. And Ali is doing the same thing now! I remind myself to have a word with her. Why do they all have to copy Sharapova and that heavy-handed baseline style?

Because she grunted and won her way through Wimbledon the year before?! What are these girls, a bunch of sheep? They should be bleating!

Halloween:

In the middle of September, stores start preparing for Halloween. By the first of October, all the decorations are out. By the middle of October, there are fresh pumpkins everywhere. Here at IMG, people put their decorations out around the seventh of October.

By the thirty-first, there is a huge Halloween party at IMG. Ali goes as a princess, Max as a three-year-old warlock. Mama X (of the X family) hangs along with her kids, and our nanny distributes candy from her unit. So do we. The kids have a good time. Halloween is a great time to be in Florida, especially as compared with France, where the weather is cold and wet, and Halloween is hardly observed.

Lance, Margie, and Aurelie are very pleased with Ali. She has made tremendous progress in the two months she's been here. Aurelie particularly has seen in Ali's game a cut above the rest in the other two groups she supervises. However, results-wise, Ali has never been brilliant: what is lacking in her game is winning: she's a great practice partner, but how good is she as a competitor? We'll have to keep an eye on this.

Our nanny is now gambling once a week and has just lost her passport over at Gio's. It has become a major issue involving the French Embassy in Miami, a certain Jean-Charles who is an envoy for the French embassy on Florida's West Coast and Tampa's French community.

November 2005

We go out with one of Ali's tennis friend's parents who, just like their daughter, seem to be very nice, not to mention quite well off. He's got a castle in France—a "tower," actually—a large house in Sarasota and a number of businesses feeding him large amounts of passive income. When we get back from our dinner evening with them, Francesca says something about our "new friends." In actual fact, as of this writing (2011), we have never been out with the two of them again.

Ali went to the final of a Super Series where she met Annie M—a Percy "student"—and got thrashed 6/1, 6/1. The good news is that she got to the final. The games were actually closer than the score indicated, but young Annie had more experience than my daughter. Annie had also been enrolled in the Academy for over a year.

The tennis clubs are fabulous here and smack of huge dollar bills. It is late 2005, and there is a lot of money in Florida and all over the U.S. The world economy is booming.

Max is with our nanny. He is very coordinated and roams about on his scooter. Like his sister, he can't stay still.

Our nanny is still dealing with her passport business and keeps complaining that her last days in Florida "are being ruined by *documents ridicules* (red tape problems)."

Throughout her stay, our nanny has been very disorganized and lost things. I think back and realize I miss those days in France with Manuela doing the cleaning, our nanny the cooking, and where we had a real family unit in a big house. However, who was footing the bill? We were.

Talking about saving money, I have purchased a racquet stringer online from Gamma products in order to string Ali's racquets. This is another idea from Monsieur X, by the way. It is a drop-weight machine and is really fun to use except that I don't know how to string racquets properly.

The first time I strung a racquet, I spent two hours and put around six knots in it. The string tensions were different—mostly loose—and it played like a trampoline, the ball coming off the strings in all different directions. The newly-strung racquet was impossible to hit with.

Clearly, I'm going to have to figure this out.

November 17-18, 2005

We went to a French Club party in Tampa. There were some nasty pieces of art by gay South American people on the wall, especially one by a guy who had infected another through gay sex, then wrote an e-mail about it to the guy and told him he had infected him on purpose! This email, projected on the wall, was scrambled, so you couldn't read it. However, every once in a while, the scrambling stopped, and it was projected in still form so you could decipher what it meant. Why put it up in the first place?

Is this art?

And how did these gay South Americans get into the French club?

Ali entered the Main Draw of the Eddie Herr as an Italian, and Gaia S's dad was jealous! Unfortunately, Ali was blown out 6/1, 6/1 by a Canadian girl of Slavic origin (what else)—Kristina B—who went on to win two more rounds in the Under 14.

The keyword is "Slavic" because most of these Eastern European girls are good, whatever country they claim as their home. Their polysyllabic name alone ending in –ova, -ic, or –ik can strike fear in an opponent.

Ali was just plain scared and could have done much better.

Aurelie and I watched the match. Ali is still trying to hit one-shot winners even though she's been schooled for years in setting up points.

I am concerned about Ali's lack of strategy, even though strategy has been the one thing she's been drilled on since she got here. Not that Nick Bollettieri is known as a strategy academy. It's known more as a "drilling academy," but I put Ali in the strategy program so she could use her brains and not just her brawn to outwit her opponents.

Unfortunately, for the time being, she only wants to use her brawn. She still hits too low, often catching the tape, and when the ball goes in, it falls too short in the court. The good thing is that she goes for everything, but there is no variation. No slice, no drop shots, no running up to net after a deep groundie for a surprise volley attack, no chip and charge or serve and volley. Just hard low groundies and once in a while a swinging volley, win or lose, depending on her approach.

It seems to me—especially in the woman's game—that the girls are just these macho groundie bangers who bring precious little "feminine" touch to the game. Just "bang, bang, thank you, hot dang," and off they go.

In my day, in boys' high school tennis and in boys' tennis today, they did a lot more with the ball in that they worked with spins and played around with different types of shots.

Simply put, boys look for the tennis in the drills, whereas girls look for the drills in the tennis.

In some ways, girls listen more to their drill masters and—no, "duh"—just *drill* while they play. Boys listen less but seem to remember tennis is a game like any other that they want to win. Hence, they use a variety of shots to outwit their opponents.

Girls just want to bludgeon their opponents off the court.

As for style preferences in tennis, I've always hoped that one day the women's game would follow in the men's tradition—from Tilden, Perry, Kramer, Budge, Laver, Rosewall, Smith, and Nastase on down in the pre-history of modern tennis to Becker, Edberg, McEnroe, Rafter, Sampras, Henman and now Federer, Djokovic, Nadal along with the younger group coming up.

The Tennis Bubble

On the women's side, there have been some excellent players like Lenglen, Goolagong, B.J. King, Navratilova, Court, and now Henin and Mauresmo—the latter two were both retired by 2010—who lead the women's game with their touch, feel and one-handed backhands.[24] But these kinds of women players were in the minority in 2005 and didn't gather a following like Sharapova, both of the Williams' sisters, and other "bludgeon bashers" had.

In fact, the only woman still playing in 2005—one with a two-handed backhand that I enjoy watching because she hits with all kinds of shots and spins—is left-handed Patty Schnyder.

Aurelie is not doing too much "accent reduction." She claims she doesn't have time, but she does seem to have time to coach Ali. And I'm all in favor of this. This is why we came to Florida. However, right now, she's teaching Ali tennis a lot more than I'm teaching Aurelie English. There's a trade imbalance here that is growing every day.

---

[24] The two-handed backhand came into wide use with Bjorn Borg in the 1970s and initially was a more consistent, powerful shot that was easier to impart topspin to the ball than the one-handed backhand. This was because the non-dominant hand created the top spin. Despite gains in racquet-making technology (racquets are lighter), many children still play with the two-hander today because they start so young and don't have the strength to swing a racquet with one hand on their backhand side. At the end of the day, however, one can do a lot more with the one-handed backhand, including imparting top spin.

Our nanny has had to leave because her ninety days are up, and she has no working visa. I had her take Max to school today as usual but picked him up myself after dropping her off at the airport. We played the French songs for children in the car as if she had never left, but I felt some terrible nostalgia as if part of Max's history had been changed forever. I know our nanny was already missing Max as she waited for the plane to take off. It was hard to feel what Max felt, but all I know is that after our nanny left, he never spoke French with us while we lived in Florida.

I got a call from our nanny who needs a business reference in France. Her future "employer" told me she seemed "bizarre," so I said she had been very good to Max, who "adored" her.

I feel sad that she has left. I feel sorry both for her and Max but especially for her. Max will forget about her in the long run, but will she forget about Max?[25]

December 2, 2005

The Prince Cup and Orange Bowl are coming up, which will mean two round trips to Miami in two weeks with family. It's a bit expensive, and Max has to miss school because of his sister. Is this right? One could argue he's very young (only 3 ½), but it really isn't right. It's just part of our family's sacrifice for Ali's tennis.

---

[25] Nanny Jocelyne died in 2013.

December 9, 2005

Ali got "bageled" (6/0, 6/0) at the hands of a Russian in the first round of qualifying. The scoreline was pretty severe. I had brought the family just to watch her play. We were back in Bradenton within hours of her loss.

Orange Bowl

We went back to Miami the next week, and Ali got beaten—again in the first round of qualifying—but in three sets this time. I was proud of how she fought hard during three long sets.

Along with the Eddie Herr, the Orange Bowl is *the* premier junior tournament in the world. Former winners and finalists of these tournaments read like a "Who's Who" of the top players throughout the modern tennis era. The Boys and Girls 12s and 14s and under divisions are held in Coral Gables, whereas the 16s and 18s and under are held in Crandon Park.

Christmas Holidays, 2005

We spent the Christmas holidays in France with Ali doing a tennis training camp with her club in Chatou. They certainly didn't give her extra help or preferential treatment because of her being in the States. Quite the opposite. As was their wont, they were even more critical of her. But she was able to see her friends, keep up her French ranking and improve her game on clay.

January 2006

Back in Florida, we went to tourneys in Pembroke Pines, but Ali's level has dropped off a bit. So has her schoolwork. Once again, Aurelie is spending a lot of time giving her tennis lessons but doesn't seem to want to commit the same time to work on her own heavily accented, difficult-to-understand English. I'm increasingly worried that our "exchange" is not working, i.e., I'm accumulating tennis hours, and I'm afraid I'll have to pay her in cash rather than in teaching hours.

Mauricio noticed Alex's arm was coming out on her forehand instead of remaining close to her body throughout the beginning of the stroke. He suggested tying her arm with a belt close to her side. We did, and it seemed to help. This is just an example of how one must constantly monitor what tennis players do so a bad hitch doesn't creep into the equation. As players play matches, mistakes sneak in and need to be addressed immediately, so they don't get over-practiced and consequently reinforced.

Ali doesn't seem to win against the girls in Percy's group: Mara, Gaia, Annie, and Nathalie B. The thought runs through my mind that maybe she's got a complex about them. Maybe they're just better, but I don't think so. They've all spent a year more in the program than Ali has. They're definitely more consistent when they play than she is.

One thing I've noticed about Percy is that he only takes on consistent players. Flashy players who can hit any shot in the book—like my daughter can—only interest Percy if he *believes* he has free license to transform them into errorless grinders.

In contrast to what I said before about style, playing error-free tennis is what it's all about, at least in 2006 women's tennis.

Ali doesn't seem to fit the equation, and that's why she isn't in his group.

My mother and sister are here for the month. Mum, who is 96, has health worries—arrhythmia—and we take her to Blake Medical Clinic for a check-up. She's ok but has to maintain her Coumadin level.

Mum's health doesn't stop my sister from buying a cute townhouse in Mirror Lake, though, just before she leaves. She doesn't know it at the time, but—as was the case for us— events later reveal that she bought her townhouse at the top of the market.

February 2006

Ali continues to train hard with Aurelie, but not so much with Lance and Margie. Aurelie is very complimentary about Ali, saying that Ali has more talent in her little finger than all the girls in her other group. Plus, there is the French thing that they share. This is the first year for both of them out of France.

As for Aurelie becoming Ali's coach, we talk about it openly amongst ourselves but is she the one for Ali? And how or even why should we take on a French girl when we left France for Ali to play tennis in Florida? As for paying people, why should I pay someone extra when Ali is already in the Bollettieri program as well as the Strategy Zone program run by Lance? Also, there is definitely a lack of balance with Aurelie regarding tennis in exchange for accent reduction. Aurelie wants to be Ali's coach but definitely doesn't want to be paid in accent reduction psychic dollars. What it translates down to is that learning to speak English properly fetches fewer dollars than learning to hit a tennis ball over the net.

As for Ali's tennis, it is up and down.

Consistency has never been her strong suit, and it appears that nothing has changed in that department here in Florida. Consistency comes from having a calm, confident mind that can concentrate on one ball for a long time.

My favorite sports team of all time—the *Montréal Canadiens* hockey team—happens to be playing the Tampa Bay Lightning on my birthday, Feb. 28th. The Lightning last won the Stanley Cup[26] in 2004, and they are a great draw in Tampa. Francesca finds this out and buys tickets for us to see the *Canadiens*/Lightning match-up.

We are becoming friends with Tammy and Manny Z in the apartment below. Manny is the coach of Ali's "Bradenton Prep" high school tennis team and wants Ali to play for the team, but Ali doesn't want to. I'm also not in favor of her playing and spending a lot of time traveling to these events because why pay for Bollettieri? There would be too much time wasted going to and coming from games. Who's paying for what here?

March 2006

We were expecting a French friend, Sylvie, and her family to come to visit, but they didn't come. In fact, no one has visited from Europe despite the fact that we have extended an open invitation to all our friends to stay in our empty apartment.

---

[26] The Stanley Cup is the premier prize for ice hockey in North America. After a long hockey season lasting from early September through late March, sixteen teams take to the ice for the playoffs, which last another two months for the winning team to emerge and take the Stanley Cup.

Aurelie, Lance, and I are at a crisis with regard to Aurelie's hours and exchanging Accent Reduction classes for tennis lessons. Aurelie tried to put the blame on Lance for his charging us too many hours, but it turns out that Lance was completely right with his hours. Aurelie should have told me about her not wanting to study English. Instead, my suspicions were confirmed when it turned out that she insisted on being paid cash for her tennis lessons with Ali.

My racquet stringing has really improved, and I am now able to string most racquets properly. I studied a free DVD from ATS sports, and this video helped me get through the aspects that were holding me up.

Ali's results are up and down in her tournaments. She is not playing brilliantly, and I feel she could do a lot better than she is doing.

April 2006

Ali's tournament at College Station (Texas A&M) in Texas was a washout: a first-round qualifying loss.

We turned down a good rent from our French house because:
1. We really didn't want to rent to someone else (suppose we needed to come back, and Florida didn't work out??)
2. We didn't want to make the effort to move our belongings out of the house. Since we changed our mind the day before we were supposed to sign the rental by fax, the people who were going to rent our place were pissed off.

In retrospect, and for various reasons, we did the right thing by not renting.

In the second half of the month, Olivier and Dominique came and stayed in our empty villa for the Easter holidays. Olivier, one of Ali's first tennis teachers and a good tennis-playing friend of mine, was impressed with the Bollettieri players and tennis program's quality and professionalism. He was also impressed with the energy of the place. Kids playing matches, trainers with shopping carts full of balls, rock music blaring on Friday afternoons, "Red"—Tommy Haas's coach known for his red hair and white, white skin—seated on his pink bicycle and screaming away, Nick with his sunglasses yelling at someone on a nearby court.

Putting my own spin on Olivier's feelings, I would add the French tennis teaching program has too much talk and not enough actual hitting of balls. U.S. tennis needs more talk, but you can't knock the drama of the place.

Ali's tennis is still up and down. She's playing a lot with Aurelie, but things behind the scenes are going on. Aurelie keeps talking about not being made a fool of. She feels that she is doing a lot of teaching work and not getting enough money for it. She throws her hands in the air and exclaims, "What do they see when they look at me?! Do they think 'Moron' is written on my forehead?!"

The next day Aurelie got fired from Lance's program, and I finally had to settle up with her—in cash—for all the extra hours she spent with Ali. Not that I minded because she helped Ali a lot, but I felt she took me for a ride as far as payments were concerned. Let's face it: The work I did with her in accent reduction never panned out and was never paid, or maybe it was her American husband who had something to do with it, or maybe she didn't feel it was worthwhile. I never understood.

Anyway, now Ali has started to work (play) with Carling S (a former world #8), and it seems to have really transformed her. Her game has picked up overnight.

Carling is a really tough coach, and I mean that as a compliment. She is reported to have said to another one of her students after the student reportedly whined, "I feel like throwing up" after an arduous overhead/volley session: "There's a trash can outside the court. When you've finished, come back for more because we still have a long way to go."

Carling's way is simple: in a nutshell, it's just Tennis 101—reacting quickly, moving quickly, and thinking quickly. She's not happy if you don't bust a gut playing for her, and at $120/hour, my kid definitely needs to bust a gut!

Carling has three children[27] who all hit the ball well and hard. Olivier only saw one of them play and was especially impressed at how daughter Carling Jr. hit the ball, but then Carling has been exposed to that kind of play all her life.

---

[27] Carling gave birth to a fourth child in 2010 and a fifth in 2011!!

The Tennis Bubble

Max is actually speaking a little French again after spending a week with Olivier's children Marie and Julien. But after two weeks in the States, it's now time for them to return to France.

May 2006

Lance told Ali and us that he had been very impressed with Ali's progress the first two months of the school year but that since then, she had not delivered—tennis-wise—as she should have. At least to him. He would be expecting much more from her during the next school year (2006-7).

Margie and Lance feel Ali is in the middle of puberty, and this is why she hasn't done so well. Psychologically, her emotions are all over the place. Physically, however, her growth rate is normal for a thirteen-year-old girl. She's grown two centimeters since the fall, 2005 (that is in 6 months). Not enough for her to not be in control of her body but change all the same. She's 1m66 now or a little more than 5'5."

Memorial Day Weekend, end of May 2006

We went to another national 14s tournament in Boca Raton, and "Uncle Bud" came to watch Ali. There were a lot of good players there, but unfortunately, she again went out in the first round.

Ali's problem is that she refuses to rally and wants to win in one or two shots. Even golf has a minimum number of shots for each hole to reach par, although the fewer shots, the better. There is no par number for each point in tennis: they can be as long or as short as one wants them to be. Ali prefers them all to be short.

June 2006

We went back to France on June 1st. Her tennis has vastly improved because she "won up" ("*perfé*" in French or "performance" means to win up) five and six ranking levels at 4/6 and 3/6, beating her friends and Ligue-trained players, Lana B and Marion T.

She wanted to train with her Chatou "friends" at the club, but all coach Emmanuel P and his cronies offered her was a low-level workout with some of the not-so-good boys. Apparently, the pros at the club (including Emmanuel P) had not been impressed enough with her when they saw her at Christmas, or else they couldn't get their heads around the fact she had left their number one competitive club in the area to go and train in the U.S.

Tennis Teachers, June 2006

As of June 2006, Ali had had thirty-one tennis teachers. By the time 2011 rolled around, the list had been extended to forty-two. Certain people would say that there were far too many teachers, but that's just how things turned out, what with our being in three different countries and all. Most of the coaches only spent a little time with her. Others spent a lot.

As I mentioned before, good tennis teachers—most of them—usually say the same things repeatedly, but each says them in his own way. Often, one way might make sense to a child, whereas another style of teaching might not.

I was always hovering in the background, making sure that grips or service motions weren't radically changed or altered.

Ali's Tennis Teachers in chronological order from 1997-2006:

1. Richard B
2. Olivier F
3. Didier E
4. Virgil V
5. Patrice M
6. Thomas P-L-H
7. Nicolas T
8. David B
9. Florence S
10. Francesco B
11. Mirko
12. Vittorio B
13. Andrea F
14. Guillermo P-R
15. Emmanuel P
16. Aurelien G
17. Nicolas L
18. Jean-Philippe
19. Lance L
20. Margie Z
21. Aurelie L

22. Chess
23. Nick B
24. Mauricio H
25. Reggie
26. Jeff R
27. Percy M
28. Julien L
29. John E
30. Carling S
31. Robert S until June 2006[28]

August-September 2006: Back to School

It's obvious that the expectations here have changed dramatically in one year. No longer can we say that it's our first time, that it is all new, and "we'll see how it goes." We turned down a significant rent on our French house because we weren't sure if we really wanted to put all our furniture into storage for three years, which would have been the price to pay if we had committed 100% to Florida—that is, 100% to Bradenton aka Tennis Florida.

---

[28] From 2006-2011, she also used the following tennis teachers: 32) Warren, the Australian Lefty -- 33) Yuri -- 34) Jose L -- 35) Sylvester (Sly) B -- 36) Giorgio B -- 37) Simone M -- 38) Isabelle G -- 39) Jean-Marie -- 40) Gilles D - - 41) Agustin M -- 42) Yuri -- 43) Irena.

Obviously, money's not the object here or the price—at least that's what I had said then. Our girl is thirteen. She's been hurt from time to time, although she's been in pretty good shape lately compared to a few years ago. Her right foot is fragile, there's her scoliosis, and her mind is scattered and not concentrated enough. I'm obviously partial, but it is my opinion that she continues to play at thirty percent of what she's capable of. Her 30% is generally good, but not with respect to the girls here who seem to give a lot more of themselves. Playing at 100% is what it's all about, but as a former tennis player myself, one has to try to develop this intensity.[29] And playing at a consistently high level is just as much of the game as hitting backhands and forehands.

September 2006

After having spent the summer carrying around a hernia, I finally decided to do something about it. Upon my return to the U.S., I saw a doctor, and surgery was set for September 16, 2006.

Meanwhile, a problem seems to have occurred. During the first two weeks of September and January, the kids have to play matches to see who goes in which group. There are three groups of girls 11-15, but they are supposedly formed by who beats whom in the "challenge" matches.

Ali won four and lost four, except that the ones she beat (except one) are not in the top group (as based on last year).

---

[29] Just to put the record straight, 100% is certainly not a level I ever reached in my matches although I did play at 90% from time to time.

So she will return once again to the second or middle group, which is fine in that anyone in this middle group can beat anyone else, so what's she complaining about? Is it her ego? As tennis itself is based on a striving towards the top, does Ali want to be recognized as one of the best?? And is she ready to work for it? Another girl she beat a couple of times last year is a big, strong girl who started tennis late. Over the previous three years, she has been in the same weak group. How long will she or her parents put up with this situation, i.e., with her not moving upwards through the groups?

9/11

It's the fifth anniversary of 9/11, and the groups have now been formed. Ali lost 8-4 to Mara on Friday, which was her "last try" to see if she had a chance for the top group. She has been relegated to the second group, which is ok since anyone in that group can beat her, and she can beat anyone else there as well.

I am at a quandary now. Do I shell out more dollars to have her play with Carling and Bollettieri stalwart Jose L like last year, and if so, how much? At this point, Ali likes Lance and Margie but do they work her enough? Whatever I choose, I know exactly how to *complement* her training by training her myself (should she even want me to help her), but right now, I'm going in for my hernia operation: Will there be enough time, and will I be well enough to carry on this training?

Not to speak of the most important question of all: How much does Ali really want to improve?

Heart-to-Heart, September 2006

Back in our open-plan living room, the three of us hash out Ali's game over lunch while Max is in school. Ali's in tears because she realizes that not only her tears but her anger on court as well as her tight playing all stem from the fact that she's not playing up to her real potential. But I feel it's not just that. When one is psychologically closed to having fun on a tennis court, one is also closed to trying out new things and rationally understanding what is going wrong.

For example, (and for years), I have been telling her not to hit so low over the net. The Bollettieri philosophy alone is: "Take the net out of play." And yet, as she gets tight, she hits harder and harder, lower and lower, and always short down the center of the court. The result: Error upon error on the tape, and when she gets it in, her opponent has an easy time of taking her short ball and making her run side to side like a rabbit.

In other words, she makes her opponent look good while she bangs her head against the wall and runs side to side.

Ali has now left the room, and her mother is furious as she comes to terms with the fact that Ali will once again be in a lower group at the Academy, but I tell her that this is just part of the game of tennis.

My wife must understand that if Ali continues to play down, she deserves to be demoted.

That is, why should she be promoted if she's playing down? One can't claim to be playing at one level if one's results are at a different level. One can't claim someone's a bad player if one can't beat that player. And one can't claim to be a good player if one is only good once in a while. All this is true of our daughter, and this is just the way it is *right now*.

Unfortunately, I must say she's inherited this from me: this mental weakness.[30] Plus, she can be physically lazy unless she's pushed by someone who doesn't let her get away with anything.

September 19, 2006

5:30 a.m. Tuesday

It is a warm, steamy morning, and it is still dark. As I always do, I creep down the stairs from our condo with my flashlight, making sure that I hold my combination walking stick/seat at the ready to club some poor crawling serpent hiding under my car or under the stairs. With flip-flops flapping, I then shuffle my way about a hundred feet over to the lighted courts, where I can hear the sounds of balls traveling back and forth.

As soon as I arrive, Ali is running far too much. She hits five forehands and backhands, runs to the opposite side of the net, and picks up the balls she hits.

"No picking up balls on my watch!" Nick yells from the sidelines. Nick has tried out a new coach on this sultry morning, and he is not pleased. The new coach was only supposed to have the kids hit but not pick up balls. They're only supposed to do that all together at the end when the shopping cart is empty.

Ali hits an easy forehand crosscourt into the net.

"Extend that arm, honey!" says Nick. On the next forehand low, she puts that into the net as well.

"Someone's gotta work on her grip with her. It's a full semi-western, almost Western."

---

[30] I only improved this part of my game later on in life. Yoga and psychotherapy helped a lot.

"How can that be!?" I ask myself. I never taught her that. Where did she pick that up?

If there's one thing I don't like as a tennis father, it's a full Western forehand grip. It has obviously come into play because of the prevalence of the backcourt topspin game. When people used to push forward to net on low-bouncing grass courts, they used an Eastern or Continental grip to pick up low balls and scoop them over the net in preparation for their volley putaways. It would have been impossible with the old game and old racquets to hit with a closed racquet face which is what the Western grip ensures. As I think about all the other coaches in the Academy that she's worked with, I wonder who let her develop this grip. How can this be? I make a mental note to take her aside after and remind her of her classic Eastern forehand grip.

Nick then takes me aside to go over some other technical points and then adds, "She's being too tough on herself when she misses. Remind me to get together with Lance, Carling, and Mauricio and go over this with her."

One year later, he actually did go over many psychological and technical aspects of tennis with her for half his usual rate. And rather than being paid directly, he asked me to donate his fee to a charity.

Only now, in 2011, does she no longer slam her racquet down after one or two swats at the ball if she's not hitting properly in practice. Only now will she hit and hit and hit until the change comes.

However, going back to 2006, I find her presumptuous to expect so much of herself when she is not prepared to put in the time to make things better. But certain natures are like that, and my daughter has this impatient nature.

Maybe, if Nick and the others had gone over all this right in the beginning, things would have been better later. And as a coach once said about her, she's not a 1000-ball grinder girl.

Drilling doesn't do anything for her.

She is lucky in that she only needs to listen and be shown the right way once and, after a few tries, she has the new technique down cold. The tricky thing is to get her to listen and be open to suggestions.

About a week later, I run into Nick again on his newly constructed blue center court.

Having noticed a prevalence of bad sportsmanship on campus, along with people cheating and swearing while playing on the fifty or so odd courts in the Academy, I go up to him as he takes a break from his teaching.

"Hey Nick, you got a second? I want to ask you something."

"Shoot," he replies.

"What's the story with all the bad sportsmanship I see around here, bad language, cheating, and swearing? It doesn't look like anyone's having any fun."

Nick stares at me for a couple of seconds as if he hasn't heard me right.

"Don't worry about that. They're havin' fun," he smiles craftily under his big sunglasses. "They're *competing!*" The word has a magical ring to it. I'm sure if I could see Nick's eyes, they'd be gleaming with malicious delight.

Then he grabs my arm and draws me closer to tell me something in secret. He motions to a couple of big signboards hanging from the fence where all the past men's and women's tennis champions who've worked out at the Bollettieri Academy at one time or another are listed.

"You see those lists," he growls, "Andre, Serena, Jim, and Maria?" (Nick is referring to Agassi, Williams, Courier, and Sharapova, respectively.) "You don't think they swore and got mad? I don't think they cheated—they probably didn't have to— but even if they did, you don't think they weren't bustin' their ass to get to the next ball, you know what that takes, in the way of guts?! Have you got any idea?!"

I nod stupidly, not sure where Nick's going with this incipient emotional display.

"They were tryin' to win!" he declares decisively. "And that's what it takes sometimes. You don't think people weren't nasty to Andre when he won at the French? You think everyone was happy that Andre won, or when Maria beat Serena at Wimbledon? Or what about when Borg was playing in Rome, and the Italians were throwing coins at him to stop him from beating Panatta—one of their own—coins they were throwing, *coins*??! We're here in Bradenton on a big campus! I can't control all the different personalities around here! Whaddya want ME to do about it?! These kids gotta go out and fuckin' fight!"

And with that, Nick smiled like a crocodile, released my arm, and waved me away.

Quod erat demonstrandum!

September 25, 2006

By this time last year, Ali had been working out for a month, and she had really progressed. This year, it's completely different as to fact and perception.

Fact 1: There has been a lot less training, and the weather has been worse. Ali's injured foot has been a real problem, but the upside is that she has done more homework.

Fact 2: Yesterday, Ali split sets with the Chinese #1 in her age category.

Perception 1: My wife had a dream about Percy and how she was trying to strangle him because he wouldn't listen to her.

Perception 2: We two parents perceive Ali to be a better player than most, and she is, but now we're much more concerned with the passage of time, how others are doing who are at the same age, and whether she shouldn't be at a certain position in the tennis hierarchy given her age and experience.

Perception 3: Someone once said happiness is not comparing oneself to others. When you're happy within yourself, you don't need to compare yourself to others. That is, "Comparisons are odious," they say, but that's the way the world works. Doesn't a big-time tournament start with 128 people and draw down to a few big names? With every passing minute, don't we on the outside compare one name to another? Spare me the clichés but remember, "If it's too hot, stay out of the kitchen!"

October 2006

We procured a piano (electric) keyboard, which is actually much better than a grand piano since it can play organ, harpsichord, etc., and it never needs tuning. Plus, one can play with the right hand only, or left hand, or even record on it. Brilliant.

We got this for Max so he could learn to play.

This is ok, except his piano lessons are costing $65/hour, which is all right if he could practice every day but does he? (We have to remember that he's only four.) The only one who practices something every day is Ali—her tennis—and even then, she needs a break.

Accounting

While I'm at it, it's time to do a little accounting in the Fall of 2006. Right now, we're at:

Max and his once-a-week half-hour music lesson: $65/session.

Then there's Max again and his daily tennis lessons at $600/month though he rarely goes, and we stopped these "non-lessons" after two months.

Next, there's Ali's tennis program at $25000/year, her bi-weekly tennis strategy sessions at $700/month, her bi-weekly extra lessons with Carling at $240/week, and finally, her sports psychology sessions with Angus at $150/hour.

Let's also not forget the cost of both kids' private schools at around $20,000 for the two of them. As you can see, people at the Bollettieri Academy think a lot of themselves, and it shows by the prices they charge for their time.

Fears: real and imagined

Ali is now showing signs of strain:
- Morbid fear of wasps/insects/snakes
- Morbid fear of cancer
- Strange questions: Will pimples become cancerous? How about that hair that got caught in the back of her mouth? Will that cause her permanent damage?
- Will her scoliosis cause her to undergo an operation?[31]

She wears a retainer at night, a back brace eight hours a day, and when she forgets to do so, she has a morbid fear of what will happen to her in the long run.

September 30/October 1st

We went to Naples a week ago, and she won four rounds in the Girls 14 to win the Super Series tournament. Brilliant! Played great! She also won the Doubles 16s w/friend Nicola! This is the Ali I know who can play, who gives the opponent no breathing room, who goes for every ball. She served at 100% for two games and over 80% throughout! Brilliant! What's scary is that this little bit of success, this little tournament, has propelled us into an "it's-hard-work-but-it's-worth-it" fantasy, and these fantasies, these little bits of success are what thrust us forward and make everything attached to tennis worthwhile.

October 9, 2006

The Ss[32] keep saying Ali has a great serve. In fact, everybody says that about her.

---

[31] From July 2005 to July 2008, Ali had to wear a back brace to stabilize her scoliosis during her adolescent and growth years.

[32] Rob S, former top 20 player in singles and number one doubles player in the world (with Ken F) is married to Carling S.

When she was a little kid, I always noticed what a smooth-flowing motion she had. Sure, the elbow was always a bit high, but basically, she had a good continuous arm movement. Guillermo P-R[33] also said her arm moved very fluidly. All they tried to do at Bollettieri and in France (with Didier E) was to lower her elbow a little bit. But believe me—especially when you look at Sampras—it is always better to have one's elbow too high on the serve than too low.

With all that, why does she lose her serve so much?

Answer: too many double faults because she—according to Carling: a) doesn't toss her ball high enough and b) doesn't bend her legs enough to go after the ball. I believe she should throw it lower but further into the court and go after it immediately as it's going up: she has to accelerate her service rhythm. Notwithstanding the quality of girls' returns today, Ali should still be able to win most of her serves.

Instead, she wins most of her returns.

We all tell her to go up after her serve, but invariably, her right side collapses as she throws the ball up. Carling's answer: "Go up after the ball and practice, practice, practice…!"

Another issue: Ali, in one-half hour from now, can go to another early morning practice with Nick. As before, it is the 5:30 a.m.–7 a.m. slot. I think it's the right thing to do because she will:

1. Be seen by Jim N as well as Nick Bollettieri.
2. She will play hard and seriously for 1½ hours with only the best.
3. She will make friends with the most dedicated players.
4. She won't miss any school, and it'll only be once a week so she won't get too tired.

---

[33] Renowned claycourter Guillermo P-R, formerly 13 in the world, worked with my daughter (mostly in the summers) from 2003-2009.

I think it's a good thing, but when I knock on her door, she doesn't think so. She lifts her head slowly off the pillow and, in a thick voice, mumbles: "Too many people, too young." Then she falls back asleep. I gaze at her and feel bad for having tried to wake her up. I almost feel ashamed of myself. It's just too much tennis. It's even ridiculous!

When Yu-Shuan, a top Chinese girl two years younger than her, was there a month ago, Ali was very happy practicing at 5:30 a.m., but we learned yesterday that Yu-Shuan wouldn't be going so early anymore because it makes her *too tired in the afternoon.*

No duh!

Knowing Nick's penchant for early morning workouts (he himself is in the gym every day around 4:30 a.m.), I asked him ironically if he didn't have a 1:30–3 a.m. slot. He looked at my poker face quizzically and then, satisfied that I was serious (I wasn't), answered me even more seriously that he had actually been thinking of starting a 24/7 tennis academy but didn't know if he could pull it off!

And this is what it's all about here at NBTA: the competition, right? I wake up to the sound of tennis balls at 5:30 a.m., and the sound only stops at 9 p.m. By now, it should be no surprise to learn that I like to see kids competing against each other rather than listening to some windbag wherever explaining the intricacies of tennis—or lounging in some European café sucking on cigarettes.

We wonder about our French friends here at NBTA. We witness Monsieur X—who has a terrible tennis style—attempting to shortcut the process by doing the teaching himself. But why live on a sports campus if one's kids do not take part in the process?

To get Ali ready for a Grand Prix tournament[34] the other day, I got out with her early, and they happened to be on the next court: The sister and brother were warming each other up with the father looking on. They could have been so good because they'd been there four years already, but because it hadn't worked out for their older brother, the father had decided to go it alone and teach what he didn't know himself.

October 11, 2006

We made an appointment to see Angus the shrink, the sports shrink. We wanted to find out about our daughter's ups and downs in emotions. Francesca ordered two books for her: The Lure of the Game and The Winning State by Philip Knight of Nike, concerning "big dogs" and "small dogs" on the tennis court.

Ali yaps like a big dog but plays like a small one.

Obviously, we want the opposite for her. What does she want for herself? Is she playing for us or playing for herself? This is one of the questions we'll be asking Angus. Obviously, she should be asking it herself.

Upcoming Tournaments:

---

[34] NBTA regularly schedules weekend "Grand Prix" tournaments which give points to the participants and which culminate in a "Grand Prix Masters" event at the end of May.

1. Angela Maria Lopera tournament on the Bollettieri Academy[35]
2. Cincinnati National 14s

Yesterday, Ali and Coach Margie analyzed a match against this Russian girl who had blown Ali out 6/0 6/2.[36]

What I've noticed and what has become almost normal is that: Ali controls the points, gets the opening, and then blows the shot on a regular basis—not just once or twice but many times. In Strategy Zone terms, she obtains "control" of the point. She nails the "hurt" shot, but she blows the (often) simpler "finish" shot. If this happens a few times at the beginning of a match, she'll also start missing serves and returns, and the whole thing just unravels. What she doesn't realize is that she is not alone, and there are many players like this.

A few days ago, she beat a girl in an inferior group 6/4 6/0. In the first set alone, she lost her serve three times.

Why? Tension. Not wanting to let go. Afraid of being unhinged! As I've said before, all the teaching pros who've seen her say her serve is a beautiful thing to watch? So why does she lose her serve?

This is because, in a match, all her muscles are tight. Thus she loses accuracy and power not only in her serve but in all her shots. How can you have any power, accuracy, or length of shot with a rigid forearm?

---

[35] Angela Maria Lopera was a good player and coach who had had a lot of influence at Bollettieri.

[36] Thanks to Lance L, the Bollettieri Academy has cameras installed on every court so that one can review any match one wants to.

She explained that her left forearm is extremely tense, which explains why she regularly hits the net. Very unscientifically, one can say that her overall stress and tension manifests itself in tight (tennis) muscles—in her forearm particularly, as well as in her legs—and tight muscles are not conducive to swinging loosely. It is difficult to enjoy any sport when you are running and performing with tight muscles.

Ali lost to Zhao Di in a team match to see if she would go up or stay put. The score was particularly severe as she made mistake after mistake while camping out three meters behind the baseline.

I did not see the match.

At least she had the guts to tell me how and where she played on the court. Apparently, she hit the ball flat and low like Zhao Di plays and like many of the other girls play today.

Except they play on or inside the baseline. We have been trying to get her to hit long and high over the net for many months, but this message has not penetrated. Her attitude afterward was particularly negative. I told her that if she continued in this way— i.e., with this bad attitude (nothing to do with results)—we would not be back here next year.

I just came across one of the diagrams I had drawn for her to illustrate what she needed to do when putting away shots. You will notice that I have labeled the two zones to the left and right of center *"jeu gagnant"* (winning game) and the middle "U Zone" *"jeu perdant"* (losing game). When Ali won matches, she would often be in front of the baseline, putting away balls to the two winning zones. When she lost, she would usually be one to two meters behind the baseline, hitting low down the center into the net or the losing "U Zone."

Ali lost to Yu Shuan, the #1 Chinese in Under 12 in China. Ali lost 6/0 6/4, a very unacceptable score, and frankly, there are just too many matches in which she is either: 1) not thinking and/or 2) too tense and/or 3) too slow. She played a forgettable first set, forgettable only in that she could have "come back," won the second, and taken the third.

However, too many sets thrown away like that leave a bad taste in her mouth and create a weak, no-confidence program. She is better than that, but does she *believe* she is and does she want to go out and "fuckin' fight," as Nick would say?

We also saw "the X Family" last night for appetizers and dinner. For people we profess not to like all that much, we seem to have a good time with them. How hypocritical is that? And why do we like them? Because they have a good sense of humor—especially Monsieur X—and we get to trash everyone together, à la française. What does that say about us as a family? And what do they say about us behind our backs after we've left?!

Once again, Giacomo M (14) won the 18 and under Grand Prix. Pretty inspiring for one so young!

Monsieur X was impressed by my racquet-stringing skills and the fact that I do the Italians' racquets: I just like to string racquets, and I earn $1500 per month on the side. Is he making fun of me or what?

October 17, 2006

I'm becoming increasingly concerned by Ali's mental state and wonder how she can possibly win anything with the emotional swings she undergoes. I believe in spending some dollars on finding out what the problem is, but not huge amounts to nurture, develop and coddle a losing attitude.

If she's got what it takes, fine. If not, then do something else. Life's too short.

My wife, who has really never played at a highly competitive level, doesn't know what it takes. Neither do I, for that matter, since I have never played top-level professional tennis, but I do know what it takes to win high school and club matches. Ali has her work cut out for her.

Right now, it is we who are reading her tennis and sports psychology books, but I think she should be the one to do so if she wants to be the player she can be. We'll see how her psychologist deals with it.

October 21, 2006

Cincinnati

Amazingly, the airport for Cincinnati is not in Ohio but in Kentucky, and it is raining hard when we arrive here late on Thursday night. I rent a small compact at the airport, and we immediately drive to the Marriott, where we get room service and settle in for the night. I fall asleep. Ali goes on MSN and hooks up with some of her pals all over the place.

Before I drift off to sleep, I think about how this girl has always had trouble accepting her identity. Maybe she's got a point. She was born in L.A., brought up in a French school with some English instruction for six years as well as in a British school with little French instruction for two years in France, then an American high school in Florida. The Italian side she clings to so ferociously is through her mother and her Italian passport, but what was her first language?

Italian, French, or English?

Answer: She was brought up with all three in equal doses. How can she now say she is mainly Italian? Not only that, she seems to hate the fact she is American, says Italy "rocks," and that she hates France.

I can understand when she says she's really not American. After all, she didn't know the following expressions upon entering the U.S. in August 2005: Pep rally, sloppy Joe, PBJ sandwich, "get served"—but why always insist on being from somewhere else? She's from somewhere else everywhere she goes.

Ali and I have been in Cincinnati, Ohio, for a day and a half. It's about twenty degrees colder than Florida, and the leaves on the trees are in that "fall color spectrum" I've always loved from my youthful years spent in Montreal and New York—from the light and dark green shades of summer to the brown, yellow and red of fall. We drive our rented car along suburban streets lined with oak, maple, and birch trees and red brick houses up to the tennis area set back on a hill in a woodsy area. A light rain makes the dead leaves scattered in front of the clubhouse glisten in the mist.

As we walk up to the club, we try to figure out how many states in the union she's been to or lived in: Florida, Texas, Georgia. But then I ask, "What about California, Arizona, Kentucky, and Ohio. (She had lived in California when she was young, and we had traveled to Arizona for a few days by car as well: "That doesn't count," she said, "I don't remember it.")

Anyway, I'm hanging out in this tennis club in Cincinnati and waiting for her to play, but I'm really thinking about our "*problemos di ricos*":[37]

- What about her tennis?
- What about the house in France?
- Where do we bring up these kids, and how does Max fit into the equation?
- We turned down a lot of Eurodollars to keep our French house open.

My central quandary is: I see a talented tennis player in Ali who is not prepared to sacrifice all the way for her sport. I must refer again to *Winning State*, the wonderful book which not only points out all the sacrifices that she needs to make but also suggests a way for her to become the player she can be and not just one who shows up from time to time to win. Does she want to consistently be a Big Dog or a Little Dog?

One of these ways is learning to visualize. From a personal viewpoint, the author, Philip Knight, teaches her how to visualize former matches in which she played great tennis and then "insert them" into her *DVD player brain* so that when she feels nervous or tweaked, she can visualize playing well.

---

[37] 'rich people's problems'

She actually tried to do this yesterday in her 0/6, 4/6 loss to this #4 seed black girl from the Midwest on whom the USTA has spent a fair amount of money trying to develop. But Ali fell short.

There are not that many good U.S. girls playing tennis today, and Ali should not turn her nose up at the USTA or the U.S. in general, i.e., speaking French or Italian in a loud voice to show off, especially when it is inappropriate: but I sense this is immaturity. I believe I did things like this when I was younger, but I could only do it in French.

Here in Cincinnati, we've been having many discussions with Mike C. and daughter Jacqueline who is Ali's sparring partner for the weekend.

One of the subjects we got into yesterday was whether we as tennis Dads were doing enough for our kids: this came about because of the "Annie" factor as in Annie M., a tremendous competitor at Bollettieri. Is she technically perfect? No! But what a heart and will to win. This is what is still lacking in Jacqueline and what needs to really be developed in Ali. The essential point is: Have we dads and mums done enough for our progeny? My feeling is "yes," and if the kid has it, she will prevail.

October 23, 2006

I tried to explain to our tennis player that:

- She has what it takes, but how much does she want to compete?
- She needs to really think about being a big dog and not a small dog on court.

The Tennis Bubble

- She played three matches on Saturday like a combination big/little dog and eventually prevailed by playing intelligently or "smart," as they say at IMG: she is still competing at only a fraction of her ability and should do a lot more mentally to be fully present in her matches.

I'm betting all my cards on her reading-digesting-memorizing "The Winning State": how to slay those terrible demons that keep her being the player she should be.

Very important: Ali also admitted that she chose not to play too well in her semifinal yesterday in the Cincinnati back draw[38] so as not to have to play Jacqueline, whom she would have met in the next back draw round. Her reasoning? I'm playing so badly that if I beat this girl in front of me, then I'll have to play my friend. So I'd better lose to someone I don't know rather than risk losing to someone I've never lost to and one who is my friend! Needless to say, Ali's mental outlook on the game needs work.

Mike C tried to put a positive spin on the whole incident by saying that all our girls at Bollettieri will receive college scholarships one day to tennis programs. To which I remarked, "Yes, but aren't we trying to make pros of these girls?"

But what's that got to do with not trying to win? And, as they used to say in the 1960s, "What's it all about, Alfie?"

October 29, 2006

---

[38] A "back draw" is a consolation draw for first round main draw losers.

It's been about a year that our nanny forgot or lost her passport at Gio's restaurant or somewhere thereabouts. Anyway, it was never recovered. This makes me think of her in relationship to Max: how much influence did she have over him?

Max's knowledge of French is now passive, but he still listens to French songs and movies and asks for Blanche Neige ("Snow White") or "Spotty"[39] in French. When you speak to him in French, though, to see if he remembers, he asks, "Why are you speaking French?"

We went out with the Italians tonight.

Our friend Carlotta really has a diamond in the rough in her son Gianluigi—we think so, though she and her husband are obsessed by their son's invincibility. What is annoying is that they don't really believe in other children's ability to play as well or better than their bright light. In fact, some people here are so caught up in their children's performances as well as their own egos that they can't even conceive of their "wunderkind" being challenged. In comparison with Gianluigi Q, I am thinking mainly of Ricky H or Mario N, who, in my mind, are great players also.

We also believe Ali is very good when she lets herself go. And so it is with most players, when they play freely, swing from the hip, so to speak. As for their parents, many have to wake up and smell the Yuban. Everyone here feels he has a diamond in the rough. The only real modest people are people like the Z family and son Jason, whom they feel will become a great college player. Jason is a terrific player with a great volley, but he doesn't stand out like some of the other juniors in the Academy because he is slight in stature and power.

---

[39] Originally in English but translated into many languages, "Spotty" is a cartoon dog series where Spotty is about the age of a five-year-old child.

There are other modest people like Rosanna and her son Giacomo, who, to my mind, truly is a diamond because he's so good. However, he would never blow his own horn, nor would she ever say he's so good to the point of denigrating other competitors' talents.

The other people we hang with here in Bradenton are the H family and the N family. Mark and Rachelle H are great people and are very knowledgeable about tennis and have a future champion in their daughter, Tammy H, who has already proved herself on the junior circuit. Mario and Nancy N are another wonderful couple who spend their time driving between the Ellenton ice skating rink and the tennis courts: their middle daughter, Hanna N, is a figure skater, while Mario Jr. is on his way to becoming a top tennis player. We parents spend most of our time trying to coordinate the kids' studies with their athletic endeavors.

Ali played a practice set with another girl in a higher group under Carling's supervision. She was leading 3-0 and 4-2, 40-0 but squandered it when they finally finished at 4/4.

The good thing is that she can do it. She must learn now how to keep hitting and forget about "hanging on" to a lead because when one thinks like that, one "holds" on to nothing.

Only by winning "match point" can she hold on to something. In other words, one never *holds on* to anything. The "holding on" concept is antithetical to the sport.

We're still trying to figure out which tourneys to put Ali into. ITFs/ Sectionals/ Designated/ Super Series: do we go to Tampa next weekend or go to Gainesville to have her play the super series (e.g., like Naples)?

Points/ wins/ what are the other girls doing, and why should we be worried about them?

What will our own girl think of our choice for her?

What do we ourselves think of our own choices?

How do we power a tennis player and make her into what she could be?

Key concept: What we're sold at NBTA is that an elite few go on to be superstars. What this means in terms of the American Dream is that we all have a chance to make it, but the reality is only 4/1000 will do so—top 100, top 50, top 20 in the ATP or WTA.

This is never spelled out.

Even our friends, the Ss—who have been in the top 10 and top 20 themselves—don't have the answer. What's happened to their first and oldest, who was groomed to be a star from Day One? Now he wants to go to college and study music.

For men, the defining concept has always been: what do you do? A man is a career, a job category—he is not even a person. In sports, the question is, "What is your ranking?" And now we're asking women the same question. In sports, this is tantamount to asking someone, "Who are you?" or "What are you worth?" We're constantly questioning ourselves as we go about our day-to-day activities.

So what happens to the others who are not elite? They go on to be scholarship players in Universities, or drop-outs, or people who quit the game on a competitive level.

When we first got here, we met a couple of them—one worked in a mattress store, one in a stationery store—who, I would say, were tennis drop-outs in that they couldn't stand the heat of competitive sport, so to speak … or did they just suffer a change of life status?

When all is said and done, though, they didn't make their athletic dreams come true because how can you compare an air-conditioned stationery office job with being a top-level tennis player—unless we're talking about "avoiding the heat?"

October 30, 2006

Talk continues to fly about how old Gianluigi Q actually is. Will he be eleven next February 2007, or will he be twelve, and why should he and his mother ridicule Ridley S's ability—a boy of thirteen who, to my mind, will be another top, if not better, player? Apparently, the Q's are really smug about their opinion of their own child, especially with respect to Ridley, and I ask myself, "What do they know, and why are they so smug? What do they have to be smug about?"

November 7, 2006

Election Day: I'm voting Democrat completely. The Republican Party is too much in favor of the Multinationals, which is ok in that I, personally, have benefited from them, but these Multinational folks are deadly afraid of raising any taxes at all to pay for things they use in great supply. The Democrats are in favor of more government control and raising taxes if need be to pay for services we all use.

We're just back from a local Tampa tournament.

Last year, Ali lost in the 14s to Annie M. This year, she went to the 18s semi-finals and lost to a lefty whom she could have beaten, but because of her temper—swearing away in four languages depending on her state of mind—she lost stupidly 6/2 6/4. Not that she didn't try, but she made too many silly errors. This match was lost by her lack of experience and understanding what to do on important points in addition to her bad attitude.

A further note on Gianluigi Q: This boy is a good ten-year-old—actually, he'll be eleven or twelve in February 2007 though nobody knows for sure—whose parents think is God's gift to tennis.

He rather proved this when he lost the 14s final of Tampa, which is a pretty good result when you're only ten or eleven years old. I didn't see the match, but this is what I heard.

Ali had to beat her friend Abby W "the Abster" in the quarterfinals. The Abster just gave up at 3/3 in the first set. Anger had made her lose in the morning, just like anger made Ali lose her semi-final that same afternoon.

This makes me think that all we talk about here is "Who's hot, who's not!"

I'm stringing more and more racquets. It's a fun and mindless way of keeping busy while listening to the TV or radio with their non-stop litany of ads.

While working this morning, I took a break and slept for a while on our yellow couch. Chatou came to mind, and Emmanuel telling Ali that she wasn't good enough last June to compete with his best girls but was too good for some of his boys. Then he suggested she hit with very mediocre players Alexi H and another guy.

And, to my shame, I told her to accept that!

As I have always been slow to react, I didn't realize it was a snub at the time. I felt bad for my daughter, yet I took it, and I got taken. Today, however, I wouldn't be so accepting.

To her credit, however, she never wanted to play at Chatou again.

It's interesting how some girls match up well while others don't. Mike C says Ali has his daughter Jacqueline's number, but then again, Jacqueline C has no problem taking care of Sara S, who poses problems for Ali. In other words, if a>b and b>c, in tennis, it doesn't mean that a>c.

Ali was fourteen on November 14, 2006. We all went out and celebrated at Jo-To's, a Japanese restaurant in Bradenton. In tennis terms, fourteen for a girl is "old." But not old in the sense of "Jennifer-Capriati-all-the-way-to-the-semi-finals-of-the-U.S.-Open-at-age-fourteen" old!

And not old in absolute terms, and very normal for a future top tennis player.

I suppose we are like all the tennis parents around here:

We try to keep our progeny as young as possible in the public eye, so they appear to be playing great at a very young age.

The Tennis Bubble

Psychological note: I am thrilled with the way Ali is maturing tennis-wise. She was devastated at losing to a guy and broke her racquet in anger.[40] But because she *was* devastated, we see that first, she *wants* to win, and second, she is aware of what all this is costing—and of course, I make sure she knows. She is doing yoga, seeing the shrink, and we talk about anger management all the time. Apparently, she has a double dose of anger from both parents.

Ali won the 14s-designated tournament in Miami—six wins in three days, and she played extremely well. She dealt with a cheating incident by cheating back—but cheating openly and obviously—provoking the other girl to call the referee.

The other player had previously and surreptitiously hooked Ali five times. Ali questioned a few calls, but nothing changed. Finally, when Ali's back was to the wall at 0-3 down in the final set, the other girl crumbled, and Ali won five games in a row, lost one, and then served out a perfect game to win the tournament. It turned out that the girl Ali beat, Madison K—a biracial whose tennis training was probably financed by the USTA—became a top U.S. professional.

I saw Ali also "win" 7/6, 3/3 against a younger boy, Augie, and drive him crazy with her tennis while he threw his racquet and swore. She seemed amused by the whole incident—for once, she seemed to see the funny side of things—and I loved the fact she was able to keep her temper.

---

[40] I am not happy with her breaking her racquet. I am happy that she cares enough to want to win.

It's very important to be able to laugh at oneself. I'm really turned off when people can't do so and take themselves oh so seriously. Sometimes, Ali has a problem laughing at herself and gets very intense or imagines a non-existent problem. Normally, this affects her game, and she'll lose—not because the other girl is better, but because she goes crazy and cannot concentrate on her own tennis.

As an example of "keeping your head when all about you are losing theirs and blaming it on you"[41] in 2006, Federer is the ultimate clutch player: two match points down against Roddick, yet it's Roddick who crumbles.

We look at a video of Ali playing her final. Conclusion (with Margie):

1. Ali has true talent and must not become a head case. She must play smart lefty tennis and show that she can capitalize on her true potential.
2. She must continue to work on her transition game, including volleys (standard and swinging) and overheads.
3. She must replay winning DVDs[42] over and over in her head to gain maximum match confidence.
4. It follows that she must really believe in herself and become truly, truly confident.

November 2006

Mobile, Al: Mobile National 14s

---

[41] From "If" by Rudyard Kipling

[42] Lance L produced a few "winning DVDs" in which he isolates Ali's winners from previously recorded matches. The idea is to watch one of these before going out on the court before a match and get "psyched-up."

You gotta wonder if we're really Masters of our Destiny here:

Ali went to the semi-finals, winning four matches but couldn't continue because she had to come back for the international junior Eddie Herr tournament[43] in which she was to play as an Italian. EH tournament referee Rick W called to tell me that Ali couldn't continue both as a USTA player in National U.S. tournaments and as an Italian in International ones. Ali had to choose. When we asked why he said it was because *certain parents* of U.S. players were not happy Ali was playing in the Main Draw Eddie Herr as an Italian while *other* U.S. players had to qualify.

We were all sorry to say "good-bye" to the Mobile tourney, but at least Ali won her four National Matches there. She might have gone on to the finals or even won the tournament because she was playing well and didn't seem bothered by a recent tennis elbow problem.

Back in Bradenton, we're all trying to find out who denounced her. I even run into Monsieur X and tell him the story. He is sure it has something to do with jealous people in the Bollettieri Academy and encourages me to write a complaint letter to the USTA. He lets it be known that—behind the scenes, mind you, he always lets me know he has discovered even more dirt than I could ever dream about behind the scenes—he plans to reveal some nasty stuff but doesn't want to tell me what it is until I hear back from the USTA.[44]

---

[43] Held on the Bollettieri Academy courts.

[44] I wrote them a note but like everything today, it was never answered. It was as if I had never spoken—a lone voice baying for naught to the wind.

Eddie Herr

Ali won her first-round match against a Serb 6/3 6/0—an excellent win—but then lost her second match 6/2 6/1 to Santa S, who was not only a superb player but also another Russian cheater. Furthermore, she was more mature and more composed than Ali. For some reason we couldn't understand, Ali continually hit to the Russian's strength: her big forehand.

Is any strategy going through Ali's brain?

You have to wonder after a year and a half of strategy. Or maybe she is so nervous that her strategy goes out the window? In most performance sports and activities, stress can knock out 50% of one's ability. It's like playing with half a deck.

I believe Ali is so involved with her own thoughts that she has difficulty casting them aside when she practices, let alone plays a match. It seems that she often plays with no apparent strategy at all.

In doubles, she won two rounds with fellow lefty, Gaia S, including a tough first round, but then lost to *wunderkinder* Annie M and Heather W—8/1—a very tough team.

In mixed doubles, she went to the final with Jason Z, and they both played fabulously in losing. They had previously beaten a great team of Croats 8/2 in the semi-finals.

Personally, I feel we're all (we parents, that is) less and less masters of our destiny here. We're just following these kids around.

December 7, 2006

Prince Cup, Miami
Anti-Semitism

An Egyptian mother put pressure on her daughter to no longer play with her doubles teammate because she was Jewish. Before that, the girls were good friends and made a decent, if not incredible, doubles team. This was after the Egyptian mother let her daughter leave with/stay with/sleepover with the Jewish girl's family. Nasty incident.

Italian Team

Ali got to know the whole Italian team that had won the Winter Cup (Boys' 14s) in Italy. They had beaten a very good French team and individually did well in the Prince Cup in Miami. We also met their parents, who were traveling around with them. Since it rained in Miami for three days straight, there was plenty of time to talk and hang out.

Ali's results in the Prince

She went two rounds in the Main Draw, beating first a Japanese, then a Croat in three sets. Pretty good, I thought. Her doubles with Monica P, however, left a lot to be desired. They lost 0 and 0 to a couple of Russians.

Then, Ali lost in her third-round singles match to a Russian 6/1 6/3.

This opponent, Maryna Z, was an excellent player who didn't need to cheat, but she did.

Most Eastern European players have to cheat because they're under so much pressure at home to win at any cost, and this girl was no exception to the rule. While serving near the end of the first set, she hooked Ali on game point and called out a ball that was clearly in (I was sitting right next to the spot on the court) with two inches to spare inside the baseline corner. Ali looked up at me, and I immediately but discreetly signaled to her that it was good.

Ali made a big stink about it, but the Russian wouldn't change her call.

So they went back to deuce, but when the Russian served a ball in the middle of the box on the next point, Ali just caught the ball and said "out." Outraged by this tactic, the Russian went squealing to one of the USTA referees. When the referee questioned her, Ali responded by saying the ball was out. When the Russian showed the linesman an imaginary mark in the middle of the box, Ali pointed to another mark outside the box.

They finally had to replay the point.

The girls continued to play with no further incident until the linesman, satisfied that there would be no more problems, left to attend to other matches.[45]

In conclusion, Maryna Z was clearly the better player that day, but at least Ali had the satisfaction of playing the Russian at her own game.

Homework

Ali now has to cram for exams because she hasn't done what she should have up to now. Let's put it euphemistically: she's been *underestimating* the amount of work she has to do. We have threatened that there will be no return to Miami for the upcoming Orange Bowl unless she spends the weekend studying and cramming.

---

[45] If the USTA or any other tennis organization used local children, retirees or other volunteers/club members **to sit in the umpire's chair** and referee a match—and paid them minimally—a lot of this cheating would go away. Official retired USTA referees who are paid $150-$200 a day to walk around the different courts usually arrive **after** the cheating has occurred.

Right now, her attitude is dismal—at least for schoolwork and tennis—and I see nothing but mediocrity in everything she undertakes unless she changes.

December 13, 2006

Tennis and school

I sent a letter to Ali by e-mail:

"You've disappointed yourself, and you've disappointed us. You should be ashamed of yourself.

Your mother was crying last night because you have no idea of responsibility.

When we ask where your books are, you say you don't have them. When we ask about your homework, you answer, 'I didn't have any.' At least you admit to doing one hour of MSN a day. Now you know where to find the time. Do you realize that MSN adversely affects your tennis as well as your school results? You must limit your time on it or do it only AFTER school work is done."

(I know I sound like a scolding fusspot here, but what else can I say?)

Orange Bowl, 2006

Disastrous.

After a long talk with her friend Juliana M[46] about appendicitis, Ali, who was hurting from something anyway, "decided" she would suffer from this particular affliction during her first-round qualifying match. As noted previously, the match itself had been rain-delayed for three and a half days, and Ali and the others had been goofing around with the whole Italian tennis team.

It's true that she had experienced some hurt along her leg, but there was no appendix problem and no other major problem, either.

However, she had decided there was. Even with Coach Percy and another coach—who had brought his daughter along expressly to watch Ali[47] as well as a talent scout from the renowned Mouratoglou Academy in France all watching—Ali not only played miserably for about twenty minutes. She also retired from her match early on, claiming she couldn't play. Now that I think about it, maybe she was right to retire since all she could think about was her appendix!

After that loss, we cleared out of Miami pronto and drove back to Bradenton. It had been the second family round trip to Miami in less than ten days. We tried to get an earlier ticket out of there back to France but there was no way. So we had to leave on the 21st as planned. We all went to the Dali Museum in St. Pete (St. Petersburg, Fl), and Ali was left to study by herself.

France, 2006

The trip to France was hell and included a four-hour electrical delay in Tampa. We couldn't leave the plane for four hours which shortened our time arriving at Gatwick Airport in the UK, so we went straight to the Eurostar at Waterloo Station in London where we boarded the high-speed TGV[48] train for Paris. Max was a great traveler.

---

[46] One of Ali's Ukrainian tennis friends

[47] This coach had been particularly impressed with my daughter when he had seen her play in another tournament.

[48] *Train Grande Vitesse*=High speed train

Ali rested a few days, and we got back to once-a-day practice sessions in her club in Le Vésinet. As I pointed out in the opening chapter of this book, she was playing and training very well and only lost one in eleven (the final in three sets) matches in France. These included sweet revenge matches against "Ligue" girls Joanna L, 7-5 6-4, and Cecile D, 6-1 6-3, girls who used to beat Ali easily.

Ali should have won the final, but there was a disgraceful incident in the Nanterre and Jean Bouin[49] tourneys wherein both finalists–Ali and Pauline L—were also scheduled to meet in Nanterre in a semi-final there. Pauline won her morning match in Jean Bouin with difficulty. Ali won hers easily. So now it was supposed to be Ali-Pauline in the final that afternoon at Jean Bouin and Ali-Pauline in the semi-final at Nanterre, *both matches at the same time*. Ali called to default the Nanterre match as she could not be in two places at once; Pauline and her father/coach told us she would do so, too. However, they sneakily disappeared and went to Nanterre. Unbeknownst to us, Pauline lost her final against one of the two other semi-finalists—Ali had been obviously eliminated as a semi-finalist by a W.O.—and then returned to Paris where Ali had been waiting patiently for two hours because the Jean Bouin tournament directors had put pressure on Ali not to default Pauline by W.O.

When they ultimately did meet in the final, and after tanking the second set on purpose because she was so tired (this was the third match of the day for her), Pauline then came back to beat Ali in three sets, 6-4 in the third.

---

[49] Jean Bouin is the name of a club in Paris which also houses the "Lagardere" group (top French players like Richard Gasquet and Michael LLodra belong to this group).

It was a shame Ali could not beat Pauline and thereby make her pay for her cheating, but overall, Ali played a great two weeks of Christmas and New Years' tennis in France.

Back to Bradenton

Once back in Bradenton, Ali continued her victorious ways with wins over "Percy" girls: Jacqueline C, Ljuba P, and Skylar K to—as I put it in French—"set the record straight."[50]

January 2007

It's early 2007, and we're off to Miami today for a 14s National.

I receive an irritating e-mail from the tenant in our other apartment. It seems that he believed or "heard" I would be painting his rented flat last summer (2006) because it had been "filthy" ever since he and his wife had moved in with their only daughter, Skylar K, last summer. There is a universal mentality in certain low-prole circles that because one *pays for something*, one can be rude and accuse people of saying things they didn't say.

To put things in perspective, what happens is that after five months of renting from me, my tenant decides he needs painting in the unit. He also says that it is filthy—it is, but it wasn't when they started renting from me—and their personal filth/untidiness has nothing to do with paint) and claims that I had promised to do this painting for him during the summer of '06.

Of course, this is not true, but he claims it is.

---

[50] *"Remettre les pendules à l'heure"*

Curiously, this complaint comes smack upon Ali beating his daughter soundly in a group match. Among other things, he claims to have been "warned" about renting from me (Percy M??)[51] and that I was a fake Frenchman with a fake "Persona" and a fake accent!

In other words, he thinks I'm a phony. I'm flabbergasted.

U.S. people may believe I'm French because I have lived out of the country for a long time and have a French last name. They also mistake my Canadian-accented English with being "foreign" and "un-American," maybe even—God forbid—French!

When we arrive in Miami—a place where everyone speaks English as a second language and often so badly it is incomprehensible—Ali and Fran have to wait in line for an hour while the disorganized tournament committee takes everyone's names. There is no draw sheet—just a short note to say where people are to show up the next day. Everything—including the hotel—smacks of low prole class and low value for money.

Percy meanwhile calls Ali *"Italiana"* as in, "Are you finally, *finally* going to be in my group now, *Italiana*?"

As if it was such a great honor to be in his group!?

Meanwhile, Jacqueline C has been "promoted" to Percy's afternoon group. But from my discussions with other tennis dads such as Mike C and Pete D, being in Percy's group is not the great thing Percy claims it is. What about Skylar K? And what about Tristan D?

Ali has beaten both these girls.

---

[51] Percy M also rented different places he had bought out to the parents of players. Maybe he was trying to steal back some of my business after I had stolen his?

The egos are unbelievable here, but what about Ali's ego?

Does she have enough of an ego to survive and to be able to deal with the politics of tennis and with Percy?

The Will to Win

I run into Mrs. E, who tells me her daughter has had so much bad happen to her that they thought Eye-Eye E[52] wasn't going to live.

Having physical setbacks like that makes one look at life differently. It makes one appreciate life more. That's why Eye-Eye's so happy to be at Bollettieri (she also happens to be in Percy's morning group) and why she tells her mother she's so happy.

I just wish Ali cared more about her tennis and studies than she does, but I'm beginning to discover that by our really wanting tennis for her that Ali seems to want it less for herself.

Dealing with her (Ali) has become impossible. At least for me, but it's also tough for my wife. Ali's attitude is so negative towards everything. Margie tells me it's her immaturity. From a tennis point of view, and in other ways as well, she's far less mature than other girls her age. Hopefully, this will change in a few years.

Sometimes I feel every discussion here is a sort of test even though it "appears" to be friendly.

---

[52] *Eye-Eye* E was a very nice girl about Ali's age who had suffered physical setbacks but who also possessed a terrific work ethic to compensate for them. I was never sure about the spelling of her name.

I used to think it was purely an American thing. For instance, if one met an American abroad or anywhere for that matter, one would have to undergo a sort of Spanish Inquisition from him in the form of a series of questions like what one did for a living, where one lived, with whom one hung around, etc. ad nauseam.

Now I realize all people do the same thing—what else can you do to reach out to one another?—and that often they don't really care that much unless they can compare their personal situation to your own.

Fran feels Ali's game hasn't progressed to that of a Mary C or a Heather W, but then they've been here already for four or five years. Ali is in her second year, and her erratic play is due to her fluctuating concentration. She's focused well for one point but then wavers for the second point. Good, then bad, then good, etc.

I believe—as do thousands of others—that the best tennis players are not necessarily the most intelligent—whatever "tennis-playing intelligence" means—but those who are genetically disposed to concentrating the longest on a particular problem. This is why those who can sit down and focus on a game like chess or concentrate on clearing their minds in the practice of yoga, for example, have a significant advantage over others who can't. In the grand order of things, people naturally gravitate to what they like to do and to what they are disposed to do. People like my daughter need to force themselves when they get older or be forced while they're young to focus for a long time on one thing if they want to do another related discipline well, like tennis.

Percy or one of these clowns around campus also said I knew nothing about tennis. This was relayed to me via the grapevine.

Jose L is a pleasant guy and always asks about Ali. My wife's and my goal is to have Ali bypass Percy's morning group and go directly to Jose's. I believe Percy feels he's some sort of Kafkian Gatekeeper who can allow people to go in and out of groups.

Further Discussions with Mike C

As Ali's results improve, word gets back to me that Percy is now blaming the powers that be at Bollettieri for not "promoting" Ali into his elite afternoon group.

As if it wasn't his decision alone?

He seems to forget that I have a good memory. And I remember he never liked Guillermo P-R, Ali's summer coach. And when does "elite" mean "elite?" And when is a promotion not a promotion?

Or is this "sour grapes" on my part?

Discussion with Bollettieri Boss Gabriel J

Of course, I said nothing about why Ali wasn't promoted. Instead, I went "fishing" for info. How did the different groups work?

Gabriel J said it was essential to be a very consistent tennis player.

A lot of the kids being trained became more consistent and eventually became "sparring partners" (in the form of *coaches*) for the kids coming up or for the better "morning kids." I wanted to find out how the grapevine worked, but he was too clever for me. I asked him about his friendship with Guillermo P-R and if he had discussed Ali, and he told me he had at the beginning of the '05-'06 year. But he neglected to say whether he had discussed her again during '06-'07. Obviously, she had failed to impress because if she had, someone would have spoken to me about her. But once again, as in so many things, I was confronted with silence.

I think Mike C can't get his head around the fact that his kid got promoted ahead of Ali when Ali beats his kid every time. But I understand that Ali's an Alfa Romeo that breaks down once in a while, whereas his kid's a Ford that never breaks down.

Tristan D believes she's the best in Mauricio's group. She did beat Ali at the beginning of the year when Ali was hurt.

Jeff R feels that the morning group is better in that the kids don't have to worry about beating each other—they can just practice new things. On the contrary, the afternoon kids have to worry about keeping their place in the pecking order.

January 22, 2007

Carling S, Jr. is at another level.

Ali lost 6/2 6/0 to her. Ali took it badly because everything she tried didn't work, but the good news was that she served at 85%. Problem was, her serves weren't strong enough, and she served too many to Carling's forehand. She must get used to Carling's speed and power. She also must adjust her game to Carling's and find a way to win.

February 8, 2007

We went to Gio's last night with the Z family. I really like them because they're so down to earth.

What is so great in Florida is that it's tropical and so warm at night, even during early February. Before dinner, and especially on a Saturday night, we'd often congregate downstairs early around 6:45 p.m. and take two cars to one of our favorite restaurants like Gio's, Outback, or Mediterraneo. The kids would attend a movie right next door, and we would chomp down on pizzas and Caesar salads. I'd usually order a Margarita or beer, and then we'd be out of there no later than 9:30 p.m. and back home by 9:45 p.m. on a Saturday night, no less!

Over at Gio's, we would run into some of the IMG coaches, parents, and often Nick himself. Rosanna and Giacomo, the Zs, the Serbian Ss, and the American Ss, Nancy and Mario, the Hs and us—we were all regulars. It was here we'd learn who was coaching whom, who was going where, and what was going to happen at IMG. Compared to Europe, the food prices were incredibly low, and the service was particularly friendly. Later on, Francesca and I would refer to these good times in Florida as "our little life!"

Ali continues to look at me strangely. I appear to bother her. Just my very existence. I guess I was the same at an earlier age with my parents. She's fourteen. What can I say? It's a very difficult age.

I talked to Rob S, who is against kids going to foreign countries to pursue tennis tourneys and points. He feels his experience as a top doubles and singles player will do the talking for him and, it's true. This is why we listen to him. On the other hand, his talk is sinister in that he is directly challenging our dreams for our kids. Basically, without saying so, he doesn't think that much of the kids he sees playing. I'm sure he doesn't believe too much in my Ali. But he's never said that.

I'm uncomfortable around people who don't share my dreams for my kids. As long as the kids have a dream—or, when they're young, as long as I have a dream for them—I am happy because without a dream—without a plan even—how can you perform?

The only sure thing I can do at this point is to understand the finances of the whole operation. Because the basis of the "real world" of tennis today is unfortunately … Well, what is it? I'd say dollars and cents!

February 9, 2007

At Gio's last night again.

Saw Nick B with Mile and Dana while the kids went to a movie. Sara, Srna, Ali, Lucia. Ali has a geometry test today.

My aging Mum (98) and sister came to see us here in Florida. Mum and I had too many Margaritas (2x each). I hope Mum is ok this morning.

Results: Went to Miami again for a designated 16s tourney. Ali won two rounds, not playing well, but then lost to a lefty in the third round. Monica P won the tourney. Ali could definitely have done better. The good news is that Ali was still able to win two rounds without playing that well.

We ran into Monsieur X and mentioned that Ali was going to her first ITF,[53] whereupon he asked if we had bought her rubbers. She needed to be equipped with those because that was when the kids "did it," and that she had better be ready. We were scandalized by this talk until we relayed it to one of the mothers. She ascertained that some of the student-athlete girls "gave head" rather than "did it."

Why have things come to this—or were they always this way?

This talk convinced me that her mother or I would accompany Ali to all her ITFs.

Guadalajara ITF

I had always heard from a neighbor of mine in California when I was a teenager that Guadalajara was a fantastic place to be in Mexico.

---

[53] An International Tennis Federation junior tournament played for points, not money.

I didn't find it so, or maybe the place had changed radically from when this man lived there in the 1940s. Emerging from the airport to look for a taxi, we gazed out at the panorama, and all we saw was a circle of giant billboards that blocked out any view beyond it. Unfortunately, that view was yellow tinged as the air was putrid everywhere along the packed streets.

When we arrived at the hotel, I went for a swim in the hotel pool. The water had the same smell as the air did and when I washed off in the shower later, I didn't feel refreshed. I smelled like the air and the water.

The park and tennis club where the tourney was housed, however, was exceptionally well kept and magnificently decorated. Groundskeepers saw to the upkeep of the impeccable red clay courts, and ball boys and court referees were present on each court. Bouquets of flowers and bougainvillea were everywhere. The people running the tournament were very kind, and the service was second to none.

Ali won her first qualifying match against a Bahamian 6-1, 6-4, and then lost her second "qualie" to Emi M, a Bollettieri girl and the number one Japanese in her age group. Ali then lost in the first-round main draw as a Lucky Loser to Andrea H 6-4, 6-4, a match she would have, could have, might have, should have won, but didn't.

Doubles: Ali went to the semi-finals with Sasha G, eventually losing 6-1, 6-2 to a top Russian team. I was very proud of them as they beat out two good teams for their first ITF points!!

Miami

Last weekend: We all went to Miami again for a first-round loss in a super series. She won in the first round of the back draw and then lost in the second round.

Maybe I will never be satisfied, but I feel her two three-set losses should have been wins in two sets.

Margie feels that Ali has to learn to compete herself out of her problems (just *play*, in other words). Yesterday, Ali came back screaming/crying that there was so much pressure after blowing a 5/1 40-0 lead to Skylar, only to *finally* win the first set 6/4! They stopped at 1-0 for Skylar in the second and were due to continue the match Monday.

Ali finally won this match 6/4, 7/5 but she didn't play well.

March 23, 2007

College Station: Texas A&M ITF

I just saw Ali off to this Grade 5 Texas A&M ITF. But it's a hard Grade 5.[54] The ones in the U.S. usually are.

Right now, we're considering Morocco (two grade 5 events), Hungary (a grade 2), and of course "La France" (a grade 4) in August (on return from Sardinia). And maybe she'll go to Costa Rica at the end of May if we don't go to Morocco.

But why are we making these decisions about which tournaments to enter? The Academy should be.

---

[54] Junior ITFs start off at the bottom level Grade 5s and work up to the tough Grade 1s.

I don't like traveling at all, but because we have young children, we'll be doing a lot of it.

It comes to mind that when I was growing up, my parents both worked and we did our sports in school or in our tennis club in the summer. Today, the parents of gifted athletic children smother them with "love management" and control what they do because the schools and clubs don't. That's just the way it is.

Behavior

There seems to be a churlish nature in most of the American kids we see here in the tennis program. The European, Asian, and South American kids are friendlier, or if they're not, they at least say "hello" or acknowledge you exist. With a few exceptions, the U.S. kids don't. I don't know why this is. Even the following story can't really explain it:

One day, a Sunday, we run into one of Ali's tennis opponents, Holly W. She and her mother explain that Holly has a match against Annie M in one hour and that she has broken a string on her sole racquet and doesn't know what to do except borrow someone else's racquet.

I tell her, "Don't worry. I have a stringer and can do it for you if you want."

She responds, and she is only twelve years old, "I usually string my own racquets."

I replied, "No problem. There are several types of string there. Go ahead and string it yourself."

She does so but has a little difficulty with my stringer and arrives five minutes late for her match with Annie M—whose mother asks the referee to dock Holly a game for tardiness. The referee does so. Holly starts off at 0-1 and eventually loses the match to Annie M.

Whenever I ran into Holly after that, she never said a word to me. The mother was scarcely more civil.

It is a very easy thing to say and hard to do, but Ali has to get over being ahead, having a meltdown, then losing. She thinks that when she's ahead 5/2, 40-0, she could also lose 7/5. This she did, to Juliana M, just by thinking about it. She then lost the second set 6-2 and the match.

I ask why she has so little confidence in herself?

It must be in our family genes, or else we have discouraged her without meaning to. Or it's in her lack of concentration that I spoke about earlier. We want to send her back to Angus M, the psychologist. In spite of Jim Loehr's book on "Mental Toughness"—not to speak of her chats with psychologist Angus, as well as our constant discussions pertaining to "Big Dogs, Little Dogs"—she still lacks confidence. From a tactical standpoint, this translates as mostly playing inside-out crosscourt forehands too low over the net to the opponent's forehand strength and thereby leaving the whole court open behind her.

Ali lost 6/3, 6/4 to Carolyn C, her second loss to this same girl. Why does she lose to someone who's good but not overwhelming? One answer is the overuse of her lefty inside-out to the open (forehand) side of her opponent, as just mentioned. Another answer is that many of her finishing shots are a mess. Even when she's not under pressure, she finds a way to hit it out or in the net. She needs to work and work on this shot, getting close to these approach shots and rifling them in with topspin, slicing them deep in the court, or just volleying them in so that even if she's nervous, she'll still be able to hit the inner rectangle.

But does she, does she really work on her approach shots? Specifically, on her inside-in shot? Do her teachers help her find this target? Losing consistently can't be blamed solely on a "fear of winning."

She needs to practice going forward and clearing the net. Despite all the tennis she plays, I don't think she practices these approach shots enough.

April 2, 2007

Ali has been playing well again—in practice.

Carling Sr. invited her to hit with her darlings Ridley and Carling, Jr., but Ali turned it down because it was Sunday, and she was tired. I don't blame her.

On Saturday, Heath noticed Ali's elbow was coming out too early again on her forehand instead of remaining close to her left side throughout the hit. I remember that last year with Mauricio, he had attached a belt on her arm close to her side so she wouldn't forget. These anomalies are some of the little things that can happen to a stroke during competition, and this is why it is very important to practice more than you play.

- Should we let her go to Texas or not?
- We think so, now that she has ITF points.
- How about Guadeloupe? Again, we think so since she has been playing well for four days now.
- Ten miles away to Sarasota? Definitely, this weekend for a Super Series.

As for her schooling, we now believe that the way to go is Bradenton Prep Online or Pendleton Online.[55] We believe she has the intellectual maturity for this. Basically, the question that every tennis parent has to ask herself at one point is this: How do you do justice to your schooling if you're always away at tennis tournaments?

April 4, 2007

People are very competitive here. This is true everywhere but especially at Bollettieri.

---

[55] Pendleton is the K-12th grade school on the Bollettieri Academy

When Fran started telling Carling Sr. about Ali's languages, and when Rob heard her talking to Max and his responding back in Italian, he was surprised. "How do they learn like that? What's her first language? What's his first language?"

Immediately anticipating a comparison with their own children's education and the subsequent recrimination later when they are alone and finding their language education lacking, Carling Sr. pipes up. "Don't worry, Rob. I'm on top of it. I'll make sure they have at least Spanish because Carling's very good in Spanish."

Later on, we receive a very warm telephone message from Carling. And apparently, "she loves Fran to pieces!" And I'm happy she's working with Ali again, but she is much too expensive at $150/hour. Or are we being too choosy: after all, Carling was an ex-number 8 in the world?!

I think her friend Julian at $75/hour is a better value for money.

I listen patiently to the complaints one mother has about the Academy because the coaches are paying less attention than she would like to her daughter. Instead of closely examining her daughter's performance and ability, the mother is blaming the very institution that has as its goal the training of future professional tennis players. On and on she goes, this coach here, that coach there …

But underneath the word noise and strong feelings, the bottom line is that her daughter isn't making it as a tennis player. I feel bad for her daughter, but I realize the coaches are trying to tell her mother where she stands!

And her daughter knows where she stands, too: Deep down, she probably knows that she does not have the right stuff or drive to be a real player.

Does Ali have what it takes? The question keeps coming back to haunt me.

Yes and no. It's just this brain of hers: obsessed with brain cancer, death, social events, and everything else other than doing homework and winning in tennis. I remind her that she has homework to do, but all she wants is to be entertained. She wants me to imitate this guy's German accent or have her mother imitate a generic Roman or Sardinian accent in Italian so that she can laugh and laugh.

In other words, anything not to do her homework.

I remember being like that: Why do we always have to leave something we enjoy in order to go do some duty-bound "task" that we *have to do?*

We reacted to all this by pulling Ali out of two other Texas ITFs. Right now, I have no regrets.

April 6, 2007

Ali is doing much too much MSN. I do not think there are boys after her all the time, but I really don't know, nor do I want to pry into, her social life.

Her tennis is really up and down, though. She's twice beaten Emilia, a really good sixteen-year-old that Ali is accompanying to a Grade 5 ITF in Guadeloupe. It'll be nice for Ali to be on French Caribbean soil for a while. She's also going with Lance and Brett.

April 7, 2007

Ali and Skylar lost in doubles 3-1, and Ali then lost in singles to Sara S 4-0. Her playing was way below the standard she had set in her two victories against Emilia. At one point, she bounced her racquet off the clay, which prompted Paul, one of the trainers, to admonish her. Essentially, he told her that it was not a great thing—even though it was understandable—to get mad.

Getting angry is only acceptable when you come right back and try to win and be competitive.

John McEnroe was excellent at this. He would become furious—"*sturm und drang*"—then calm down, breathe and produce winners and shots of genius. The key was that he calmed down and breathed.

Lesser players forget to do so. They just remain angry, throw their racquets and give away three points in a row (which is what she did).

Paul also said that Ali is a wonderful player with lovely hands. And you can't teach hands. You either have them or you don't.

He was impressed with her workout with Carling today and thinks she will become a great player *as long as she works on her game*. All great players work on their games, but not all have the hands to start with. Will Ali be a great player? The question keeps popping up. You need the mind, too. Actually, you need the mind the most.

We went to dinner tonight. Carling showed up with Sandy and Skylar, and we all ended up at dinner together. Carling reiterated how being at IMG was such a great experience for us parents as well as for the kids. She again told Francesca how she "loved" her!

Giacomo played very well against Nicole V[56] today, 6-0, 3-6, 3-6 in a loss, but I think he'll win tomorrow.

April 8, 2007

I wrote a letter to Angus today (Easter Sunday) expressing my concern about how Ali has a fear of winning—how often she blows leads when she's ahead and how she's a hard worker, but she plays without a strategy and a workable plan.

April 15, 2007

Another dinner at Gio's, this time with Tammy and Manny Z, followed by one with the Ss, who took their place beside us after the Zs left. Funny—all we do is talk about our children.

---

[56] Still very young today, Nicole V was top 20 in the world in 2007.

Apparently, their son Jason went on a weight-training program rather than go to some California tournaments. Rob S told them: let their son build up his strength and weight but don't let him miss tourneys like Carson and Easter Bowl, the crème de la crème of junior tournaments. Rob couldn't understand why a player would forego a tourney in order to lift weights and get in shape.

I see his point of view but also see the Zs. Why go to out-of-the-way tournaments when you're not in shape? Carling believes you should be able to win two or three rounds in a tournament, or else it's not worth going, especially when you're not prepared. And especially when traveling to foreign parts.

April 17, 2007

Big Day for Ali today in Guadeloupe, where she is the #2 seed in the tournament. She needs to play the girl who beat Anne-Sophie P, a girl who was equally ranked with Ali a few years ago in a TCBB international Christmas match in Paris. I am worried about Ali's mental state, which can undo her at any point if she allows it.

However, if she learns to vanquish her fears by focusing on the ball and only the ball, she will be ok. This is easy to say but hard to do. Even so, I am worried that she is becoming a "head case."

For the record, Ali and Emilia lost in singles but won the doubles. However, they lost their entire luggage and only got it back a few days after returning to Florida.

Our daughter is long on hands and talent but short on maturity, mental fortitude, and movement/concentration. At least she's got something, but is it enough? Right now, it doesn't seem to be.

How much is this costing us, or how much are we spending per year?

$120,000	U.S. living expenses
100,000 (€60,000)	Europe living expenses
50,000	Tennis expenses
50,000	Insurance/Schools/Miscellaneous
$300,000	**TOTAL**

April 17, 2007

Max is showing that he can really play soccer: he scored seven goals in a small scrimmage, and the coach and several parents were impressed with his skills. What was striking was his ability to dribble and hold on to the ball. Since he already knows how to pass, he should become very good. He also knows how to follow directions.

April 22, 2007

Max has shown he is good in martial arts as well. Francesca will be taking him this week again to see how he likes it.

Lance has suggested taking on Ali and Emilia as his next two big projects. He said in an e-mail that when Ali first arrived in Guadeloupe, she was immature.

Now, she commands his respect.

And this is a wonderful thing for a father and mother to hear. But has her tennis level and fitness kept pace with this *newfound maturity*? Has it really changed? Especially since she didn't win her singles but "ran out of gas." Why does she run out of gas? Why doesn't she jump rope daily to stay in shape? Doesn't she train every day for these extreme conditions?

I received a great e-mail from Lance that put the blame for Ali's loss on (in no apparent order): nerves, a lack of a slice serve, *playing* opponents' out balls (instead of calling them out), not putting in a first service, and generally, *a lack of real belief in herself.*

Lance feels he has a specific plan for her confidence problem as well as an overall plan for her tennis.

My feeling about everything is "questionable." I question the following:

- How coddling should we as parents be towards her?
- When will Ali be in good enough physical shape to fight three hours through the heat and not be overcome by it?
- When will she stop giving balls (points) away?
- When will she keep her equipment in order (sun hat, cream, water, etc.)?
- How will she deal with cheating?

And I have another question:

- Can we really trust Lance, and how much will it cost?
- I feel he likes Ali, and he believes in her ability to play, but how much will it really cost?

Here at Bollettieri, we're constantly up against this question.

I asked Lance about his long e-mail to me, and he said that at first Ali was juvenile, but at the end of the trip to Guadeloupe, she had matured and had won his respect. She was the one he wanted to put into the pro tour along with Mallory and Emilia. In the searing heat of Guadeloupe, she had done her utmost to win. She had a lot of "natural talent" and was becoming a "warrior." She had fought hard through three sets and lost.

Percy

I have now had confirmation that Percy always liked Ali as a player but was put off by Yours Truly, who didn't want her strokes changed.

Somehow, I don't buy this at all.

Let's put it this way: If he had really believed in her like he says he had (he never spoke to me, by the way, but to my wife), nothing would have deterred him from that goal, i.e., being Ali's coach.

The fact is he likes to be liked, and knowing that we did not like him bothered him. Also, he likes his ass kissed, and we never kissed his ass. That also bothers him. I'm not planning to kiss anyone's ass.

And while I'm talking about Percy—and I'm not accusing anyone here—I still wonder who told our tenant to not rent from me.

And I still ask myself who wanted Ali pulled out of the Eddie Herr tournament last fall?

The Tennis Bubble

Random Facts from the Spring of 2007

- Ali is still going to bed too late
- Max played great soccer again last night
- The past participle continues to go the way of the dinosaur in IMG, Florida, e.g., I hear people say, "I would have *"went"* instead of "gone!" He could have *"gave"* instead of "given*"* it to me if he *"woulda"* wanted, instead of "had" wanted. I would have *"took" instead of* "taken" it, etc."
- Ali is working on her one-handed slice.

We're going to Europe for the summer so she'll need to work on:
- Her slice and approach
- Doubles drill along the diagonals
- Volley-Smash drills
- High over net consistency
- Change of Direction
- Deep and Short balls

April 27, 2007

We all went out for Fran's and Tammy Z's birthday to "Fred's" in Sarasota. The two Tammys and Carling were there. Lots of talk:

Carling, Sr.: Her daughter is brilliant and plays well, and she's ready for college and college tennis. Carling Sr.'s thinking of a big tennis school like UCLA for her daughter, though.

Tammy Z: She is grooming a college player in Jason.

We: We're still thinking "professional" for Ali but are we kidding ourselves? I feel we're still frozen in time. That is, she's fourteen now, but when she's fifteen, the time constraints become tighter. And at sixteen, in Rob S's words: "She's got to be a phenomenon!" Otherwise, forget about a *professional* future.

May 12, 2007

Carling's been gone for a while. First to Canada, now to New York City. I think Julian, her German alter ego is very good, but Ali has not been pulling her weight practicing with him, and her attitude has been deplorable as well.

Two days ago, Max had a huge birthday party with all fifteen kids from his class coming except for one boy who forgot about it.

The team of Ali-Sara won their three doubles pro sets yesterday for the tournament. They play at 9 a.m. today.

Doubles continues to be a poor second sister in pro tennis and pros-to-be tennis. You get ITF points, but not that many compared to singles.

It's a shame Ali didn't win her first-round matches in Guadeloupe/Mexico. She would have had a lot of points. She constantly doesn't perform "big" when she really needs the points. She still needs to:

Learn to keep her opponent off guard with big lefty crosscourt shots to set up *the occasional* inside out into the righty's forehand side a la Nadal. She still has to work on a foolproof crosscourt forehand. Why does she always let her concentration lapse and miss into the net?

Ali is only an alternate in Morocco (4th alternate) and not even a qualifier because of her 1460 ITF ranking (May 11, 2007).

The thing I'm trying to get across to this girl is that she can do her homework *as well as* tennis and do both well. She, however, wants to play tennis and *socialize*.

I understand she's a youth, but what is her job?

Rules of IMG for Tennis Parents[57]

Never talk to an opposing player's parent during the player's match.

When meeting someone you like, say "How are you?" the first time you meet, which is the same as "Hi." The second time, smile pleasantly. When you meet them three, four, or five times afterward on the same day, don't smile but rather look straight ahead and pretend you don't see them.

For people you don't like: Never acknowledge their presence.

For people you're indifferent to: Say "Hi. How are you?" or nod depending on physical proximity.

---

[57] These are obviously my tongue-in-cheek rules for dealing with many but not all tennis parents.

Never give the parent of an opponent time to talk to you about the match your children are *about to have*. On the other hand, let them talk to you *afterward* if you feel so inclined.

June 22, 2007

ITFs in Copenhagen and Aarhus, Denmark

We arrived in Denmark on Sunday, June 17th. I had never been to Copenhagen before and was impressed with the classical music being played by a pianist in the main airport lounge upon our arrival. Outside was sunny, and I was in high spirits as we took a taxi first to the courts to sign Ali in and then on to the hotel. On the way, however, I asked the driver to stop off at a store and was almost clipped by a racing cyclist as I stepped out of the cab into the rain that had begun pouring down. There are three parallel "lanes" on each side of the street in Denmark: One for pedestrians, one for cyclists, and one for the ever-present automobile. The one for cyclists was in the middle, and I almost found this out the hard way.

After eating a marvelous "bio" breakfast in the players' hotel the next morning, Ali went on to lose 7/6 6/4 in her first-round main draw match and 6/3 2/6 1/6 in her first-round doubles with Sara S. They were ahead 5/0, then held to 5/3 and squeaked by to win the first set 6/3. Their goose was cooked, however, since they really didn't play well to get through that first set. After that, they stayed back and let the other Dutch girls take over the net.

Ali tried to make a difference in the third set by going to net and being aggressive, but it wasn't enough. She has to understand she can't fire balls at the net girl over and over again and expect to win the point. She did this at least six times and got burned every time. In all fairness, her partner had no idea of how to play doubles, and this makes me wonder what they teach them at Bollettieri.

As for the singles, she was ahead 4/1, 5/4 in the first set, and both 4/1 and 6/4 in the tie-break and still lost it 9/7. Thereafter, she lost 6/4 in the second (and she was even down by 5/2). Her opponent played well, but Ali made tons of mistakes.

The gossip continues: Sara S will play a few ITFs, then try and play the challenger series. This might be the way to go for Ali, too—that is, she would go right to the second-tier pros rather than "waste" time in junior ITFs. Sara S's mom wants Sara to spend as little time doing junior ITFs as possible. Which way is the right way?

Jennifer R: Ali has a new friend in Jennifer R, a '93 highly-ranked Brit who has beaten top players (in 2007) Marie M, Chloe B, and Annie M, among others. Looks good for Ali, at least as practice partners go.

Maturity? Ali and I had a long discussion yesterday about how others' opinions are very important to her, how she changes accents to "fit in" with others, how she'll wear the same clothes, eat the same food, etc., to fit in. She wants to change all this and is aware of her faults. She's really listening to me now, and I've told her not to make fun of me in front of others because it only makes her look bad. As for me, I don't care what her acquaintances think of me. We're here today, gone tomorrow. She seems to agree with me. However, she still changes her way of being when other teenagers are around, but since we had our little chat, she seems much better.

June 25, 2007

What needs to be done tennis-wise?

- Work on a slice backhand with *one* hand
- Work on her slice backhand approach (check balance)
- Work on a backhand volley with *one* hand
- Consistent serve: should be much more of a weapon

Movement:
- Backwards and forwards movement (instead of just lateral)
- Work on her crossover movement—light feet

Mental and Anticipation:
- Try to concentrate on her *Intention* of Winning
- Everything related to *Intention*. For example, she must work on the anticipation of her "next" shot instead of admiring the shot she just hit.

Game plan:
- Systematically attacking an opponent's weak side so as to set up the put away against the strong side or vice versa. Attacking/wearing down the opponent's strength so as to put the ball away against the opponent's weakness.

Focus on Tennis/Focus on Achievement:
- Change her focus from "What do others think about me?" to "What can I do to achieve the desired result?" Both on the tennis court and off.

If we consider, for example, that the definition of happiness is not comparing oneself to others and being happy within oneself—and Ali has always said her goal is to be happy—then she should "do" things to make her happy. Whether we like to admit it or not, happiness is "an achievement goal" in however way we want to define achievement: "To do is to be, right?"

For example, in school, Ali's goal should be to learn because learning gives you happiness. For her social life, her goal should be to feel good with others, yes? And it follows that in tennis, her goal should be to try to win by playing well. In this way, if you really *try* to win and play well—and I mean *really try*—you don't feel bad if you lose because there was nothing more you could have done.

As for what I would want for her—whatever this means in the big picture—I would like her to be a leader of others.

Here's a problem. Aside from typical teenage girl preoccupations, an inordinate amount of her time is still spent worrying about:

- What I, her dad, look like when I'm with her so that I don't make her look foolish.
- What *is* foolish, and appears to be foolish in the eyes of others, whose eyes have now become her eyes.

In the meantime, this immature behavior is reinforced through hours spent on MSN Messenger, although once in a while, there is a breakthrough like when she sat and listened to me the other day. It's not like I have an inordinate amount of wisdom to impart. It's just that she has trouble breaking away from MSN (fantasy) to talk to me (dour reality).

Conclusion: We're in this tennis thing for at least another year with ITF tourneys, online study, and traveling.

June 29, 2007

Aarhus, Denmark

To complete Ali's disastrous trip (tennis-wise) to Arhus: Another 1st round defeat in singles (6-3, 6-0) to a top German junior, along with a 6/0 6/2 defeat in doubles.

Maria M, Ali's Irish doubles partner, downed three beers the night before. Ali was ill (with a cold) but still managed to go to bed too late, nonetheless.

To no one's surprise, they played terribly the next morning.

Maria M was more off her game than Ali, who—to her credit—tried different doubles tactics like net rushing and poaching. This in contrast to the stodgy Maria, who camped out on her baseline without moving, all the while hitting to her opponents who easily put her balls away at net. The only amusing incident was when Maria went to fetch a ball outside the court and stepped in thick mud caused by the previous night's heavy rainfall. At 6/0, 5/2 for their opponents, it took fifteen minutes to clean her up and one minute to finish the match.

July 11, 2007

From the cold and rain of Denmark to the heat and sun of Sardinia, Ali found herself in the Sardinian National Championships. As my wife is from Sardinia, and we go there every summer, it was only natural that we become familiar with the top-level tennis scene on the island.

The tournament in 2007 was held at the Geovillage Tennis Center in Olbia, a place where Ali trained every summer. When Guillermo P-R arrived there in 2001, he brought in some very good players, including fellow Argentine, Mariano Puerta (French Open finalist losing to Rafael Nadal in 2005), Felix Mantilla from Spain, Eduardo Schwank from Argentina, and Francesca Schiavone (French Open winner and finalist in 2010-11). These players did not train there all year round but went for two weeks at a time to prepare for their various tournaments around the globe.

Geovillage was thirty-five kilometers away from our house, and we would make the drive every day for Ali's tennis. Guillermo P-R would work her very hard on the red clay every summer.

Campionnati Assoluti Sardegna

1st Round, Ali defeated Arianna M 6/1, 6/1, and since she's had close matches with her before, Ali has obviously taken a step up during the previous two years. I watched the match with Coach Guillermo in the background, and since the outcome was not in doubt, we discussed psychology: Ali must remain positive throughout her match, and we parents and coaches should not ever say, "It's incredible" (*è incredible*) when she wins!

In other words, even though she was to win six times in a row, I should never say, "It's incredible." No! Guillermo insists. It's normal that she win, and it's negative to say, "It's incredible." Every point is the same, and when you think about it, even Roger Federer's winning Wimbledon is just another point, just another win. To go to the next level, to become really good, Ali—just like Rafael Nadal—has to treat every point just the same, whether it's a sitter, an easy miss, or a screaming winner. These points are all part of the zero-sum game that is tennis.

There is also the hidden fear of losing, which is always present but can be dealt with by tanking ("I'm better than this player, but I don't feel like proving myself today, and I'm not going to try and if she wants this win so bad, she can have it, but let there be no mistake, everyone watching can see I'm obviously the better player, etc.") or finding someone or something to blame. "It wasn't really me. It was my serve—or the weather, my father, the opponent's father clapping for her, the way she looked at me after that point, the way she cheated after I hit that winner. No one will ever understand what I'm going through. My friends must really think I'm playing badly, etc., blah, blah, blah—" ad nauseam!"

In the next match, Ali lost 6/2, 6/2 to Francesca R, an Italian ranked 3.5, the equivalent of a 1/6 in France or 5.5 in the States. This 3.5 had a good volley and smash. She put in many first serves and had a decent return, but her court movement was very limited, and Ali didn't take advantage of it—at all! Plus, there were three or four games at the beginning where Ali held game points at 40/15 or 40/30 and just made unforced errors. Then the telltale signs of Ali's poor play started to appear: Her low trajectory on balls just skimming *over* the net now landed *in* the net. Or they turned into easy set-up balls landing in the middle around the service line. Her collapsing on her first and second serves produced fault after double fault. Not hitting any of her shots with spin, especially her serve. Her hitting the ball any old place in the court and not aiming for a spot. Basically, her finding a way to lose.

For instance, at 0/40 for Ali in the first game, second set, Ali made four easy return errors in a row and then presented Francesca R with a gift: an easy sitter in the middle of the court that Francesca R put away for a game she clearly did not deserve.

Our tactics now are just to brainwash Ali with what she does right, even though she may be playing the whole match badly. This is very hard for me to do—for Fran, too, I imagine—but it's something I have to do. My greatest fear about using this tactic is that she'll just believe she's doing ok and will slide into mediocrity.

Analysis of yesterday's matches (from July 11, 2007)

Alessio and Ali won their doubles with a tremendous come-from-behind victory 6/3 in the third. This was a very good sign, and both players showed great presence at net against a terrific team from TC Cagliari.

As for her singles, she lost 6/2, 6/2 to a certain Marina. Ali's post-match analysis of her loss to Coach Guillermo went like this: "My parents just talked about Marina being the star of the tournament because she went to the third round, and this spooked me!"

Guillermo's conclusion: Ali isn't in reality. She only listens to negative critiques but never listens to positive ones. After the match, she gave some lip service to the merits of the other girl, but she's not able to analyze her own matches objectively. She said she, herself, "sucked." Her forehand, backhand, serve and volley all sucked. How can anyone win with that dismissive attitude?

Conclusion: We, Fran and I, have to be very careful how we speak to her because she's always reaching out for something negative to hang her hat on. I don't know what Fran told her, but I told her she could have moved the girl around much more than she did since basic movement was the girl's weakness.

Is making this kind of observation finding fault and criticizing her?

July 12, 2007: Back on the Practice Courts

We're up at 6:30 a.m., in the car at 7:30, and on the court by 8:30 after a half-hour drive, another cappuccino, and blah-blah-blah with Guillermo. Even at 8:30, the heat is brutal, and by 10:30, Ali is covered in sweat, and I have finished two 60-minute tapes filming her.

Her practice was good today, but it took a little work to get it together. She was only hitting and running very well at the end of the hour because she had been so tired at the beginning!

How can she be so tired after all the work she's done over the last two years? She's not having her period, so how can this be? A possible explanation: she goes to bed too late!

Tomorrow, it will be one and one-half hours on the clay, Guillermo assures me, but she's got to put in the work. I find it personally embarrassing to have a kid with a tired attitude and movement problem.

Especially when it's all in her head.

The same question keeps resurfacing: Either you want to play, or you don't.

Does she *really* want to play?

July 17, 2007

Guillermo noted that Ali's tennis was very good yesterday. He really moved her around a lot, and she was striking the ball cleanly. He was obviously trying to push her to her limit and make her go a couple of balls more.

In this way, he noted, in a match, she'll run down that extra ball, she'll get that extra point, even when she's entirely exhausted.

He also noted that "She's probably not used to working like this every day." So I ask myself, "Why not? Why isn't she!? Why is that not required at the Bollettieri Academy? Why do we have to hire private coaches to get her to play her best?"

July 21, 2007

The last day with Guillermo before going to Ireland was awful. Ali did not move her feet. She was up late the night before at the Ali Baba restaurant. We did not tell Guillermo this, but it was evident from her performance. And this was our fault since we let her come with us. The question is how to get a good performance out of her when she's tired?

Trip to Ireland

Donnybrook Int'l ITF – Grade 5. Ali is seeded 5, and coincidentally, she is staying at the Conrad Dublin in a five-star hotel. She's making this first trip on her own and was met by Lance and Brett in Dublin.

When we talk to her, I worry because all her conversation seems to be about a certain "Marius" (whom she met at the Sardinian "Campionnati") or a blond-headed guy (whom she met at the Copenhagen tourney). There is absolutely no talk of tennis, but, as my daughter and wife both tell me, I have to lighten up! This is what being a teenage girl is all about.

But I really don't lighten up because I ask myself: Is this all worth it? Where are we going with this girl? What is her level of play? How much does she care? Does a win or loss mean that much? It's not that she's playing for money, but she'll have to eat in the future, so she'll need some way of making a living, yes?

Results:
1. W 6/4, 6/1 in first round
2. W 6/3, 6/3 in 2nd round
3. L 3/6, 0/6 in 3rd round

Doubles:
1. W 6/1, 6/1 with Emilia in 1st round
2. L 6/3, 3/6, 3/6 with Emilia in 2nd round

As far as results go, not a bad tourney in that she had a tough convincing second-round singles win. Her first match, although easier, was noteworthy in that she had to overcome her nerves and the other girl's good first serve to win. Her 3rd round match (quarterfinals) was even until 3/3 in the first, at which point she lost her serve. Then, she gave up at this point, confessed she didn't care, tanked the match, and got balled out by Lance about it.

How can you play even with someone and then "decide" you're not good enough and just cave? That mentality is anti-competition, anti-tennis, and anti-spirit of the game. She must learn to compete and go for every ball.

And what are we, the parents, supposed to tell her besides putting a positive spin on the whole thing? After all, we're not allowed to say, "could have, might have, didn't!" So instead, we say, "Great! For your first two singles and first doubles match wins! It's a shame about your third round, but you'll get there as long as you work on competing better!"

On another note:

Dear Ryanair: Our 14-year-old daughter, A. Bonte, took Ryanair Alghero-Dublin-Alghero direct July 20th with a return scheduled for Friday, July 27th.

It was her first-ever trip alone.

As she was about to board the plane for her return flight on July 27th, she was pulled out of line by security and told she could not board with potential "weapons"—her tennis racquets—as these could be used as such in a hijacking.

How can an airline allow tennis racquets to be "hand luggage," change its mind, and then pull a 14-yr-old out of line and send her back?

Brett, who had accompanied her to the airport, was unreachable and was on his way back to the hotel. Lance hadn't gone with her, and his stepdaughter was God-knows-where. When I spoke rudely but firmly to a certain "Maxine" of Ryanair about this, she blamed security and said it had nothing to do with Ryanair because Ryanair had allowed Ali to board with the racquets. "Security," on the other hand, "had its own rules." I pointed out that tennis players always kept their racquets with them because the string tension changes if the racquets go in the hold. I started yelling that tennis racquets and musical instruments were the same, but my tone of voice annoyed her, and she hung up on me.

The long and the short of it was that Ali had to return to the hotel by taxi, spend an extra night and fly off again the next day by Ryanair to Stanstead in London, where she boarded a connecting flight to Alghero on Saturday afternoon. The cost of it to me was an extra €250.

Now she says she'll never fly alone again. But I say, "Never fly Ryanair!" How can Ryanair be so gutless as to use a security company for its own protection and, when things go wrong, say it is a separate entity from Ryanair? How can Ryanair do this to a fourteen-year-old girl who had only flown alone once in her life before?

I considered suing Ryanair, but it would have been a dodgy case—"Why did you let Ali fly alone? We can't control our security company"—and very expensive for us.

Holland Tournament: Aug. 13-20, 2007

A disaster. We just finished attending our niece's wedding in Brittany in France on August 11th. Ali and Fran left two days later for Holland, where Ali suffered two first-round losses in singles and doubles. First, she lost 6/0, 6/2 against a good but not insurmountable Russian. Then, she played doubles with a slightly more highly ranked English girl called Julia H, and they suffered a 6/3, 6/4 loss to two good Dutch girls. Needless to say that this was another terrible tournament because Ali was tired and didn't play well.

Clermont-Ferrand, France, Grade 4: Aug. 20-25, 2007.

It has rained hard here every day, and Ali hasn't even started yet in this clay-court tournament. We've been here three days, and she just practices indoors with me or with other girls like Cristina S![58]

Victoire M lost in the second-round qualifier, as did Jessica G—a nice girl ranked "O" from Ali's old club, Chatou.

Both girls have been very kind to Ali, but Ali is now so upset with all these conversations flying around about "who's good, who isn't, who beat whom, etc.," that she can't think straight. Yesterday, she called her mum who's with Max at home and cried a little, so I told her simply:

"Thoughts are deadly when thrown into a tennis match. Who's better, who's watching, what will happen if I don't beat this girl, I didn't like the way she looked at me, she doesn't like me, they all know that and on and on. It's hard enough being focused on what to do in a match, let alone keep track of all these distractions."

I tell her, "Don't worry about the Italian guys and what they think of your tennis." But this is easy to say and difficult to do when you're fourteen years old and in the middle of a meltdown.

I'm watching her bolt away from her game plan and realize she's hurting herself, but there's nothing I can do. I can't stop her dwelling on these clowns as the first set slips away.

Now we're in the middle of the second set, and she's talking about getting a hairband! And, of course, she does need to keep her hair in place on the sides. But why can't she think about these things before the match instead of during the second set?

She has lost in both singles and doubles, the tournament's over for her, but still, she's thinking about one more year at Bollettieri and a private coach for the next school year.

I'm not so sure.

---

[58] Cristina, a real user, had been a thorn in our side in the Guadalajara tournament ITF last January 2007. Nevertheless, Ali was still friends with her.

I feel she should travel with one of us and go for "stages" or short training programs like she does with Guillermo. She could conceivably be based in France, do her U.S. work online, and then continue with the CNED[59] program to keep up her French. We would only rent one of our Florida units and go back and forth to Bradenton. I'm going to try and build up an Accent Reduction business as I did before. Keep an Internet and U.S. business and work in both France and the U.S.

August 23, 2007

As we drive away from Clermont-Ferrand, I think about Ali's desultory results, and a thousand thoughts are going through my mind. First of all, she lost to a good Dutch 1993-born girl in the first round called Loomans with a terrific one-handed backhand. The score: 6-3, 6-4. Then, with partner Cristina S, there was a second doubles loss 6-0, 6-4 to the French pair Alizé L and another girl whose name I can't recall.

I'm depressed because:

1) I don't see her really wanting to change her attitude towards tennis. And her attitude towards school is very negative. And she seems to be doing a lot of MSN.

2) Apparently, according to this Italian coach I met at the tournament, "I am stressful" (that is, without knowing me—we talked briefly once—he believes that I, myself, am a stressful person). Apparently, he is said to have said this to Ali. Am I the reason—and excuse—for these losses?

---

[59] Centre National d'Education: France's National Education Center correspondence studies program

3) The doubles match was played in a state of hit and giggle. Can't they giggle *after* the match and still have fun? Isn't doing something seriously—playing really hard and either winning or losing—even more fun than mucking about on the court, or is this my doom/gloom attitude at work?

4) Personally, after a couple of losses, I would:

       a) Start serving buckets of balls to get my game together or,

       b) Start working out instead of socializing.

Is this behavior typical of a fourteen-year-old, and is it typical of a tennis player? According to Emiliano R (Antonio Z's coach whom we met in Copenhagen), "Ali is a good player who needs to grow a little—meaning becomes a little more mature."

Where, if anywhere, do I fit in?

Basically, what type of kid do you have to be to fit a top player's profile?

People did warn me throughout this ordeal not to give too much and not to expect too much from her, but this is hard to do when you're going through the process. I'm not on the court myself, but it is as if I am—after all, where are her coaches? It's not like they're here on the court with me right now or that they care about her. Where is Guillermo? It's easy to criticize me, but who else is here doing the heavy lifting but my wife and me? And when it's your own kid they're talking about, it's even tougher to put up with.

After all, the kid is just a chip off our old block.

One tends to think from one's own perspective: what would someone who really wanted to play tennis do? And the answer is she doesn't seem to really want it enough for herself—at this particular time—but this is hard for me to admit.

My attitude as a player was to really go for it, but I was not as good at fourteen—for a boy—as she is today, and obviously, I am not my daughter.

September 23, 2007

It's been one month since my last journal entry.

Ali started school online at Bradenton Prep and is already behind in math.

She is leaving for an ITF in Atlanta.

Ali is very up and down and spending too much time on MSN, but what can I do, ban her from using it? The school requires her to do all her schoolwork on a computer!

The morning program is quite good, but there is too much exercise. I'm worried about her burning out:

6:30 –7:30 a.m.	Running
7:30– 7:45 a.m.	Snack
7:45–10:00 a.m.	Tennis
10:00–11:00 a.m.	IPI[60]
11:00–noon	No homework/lunch
Noon –1:00 p.m.	Margie/Lance Tennis

---

[60] International Performance Institute is another term for hard exercise!

	Extra	5-mile run when Ali is in town (not at a tournament)[61]

Right now, Ali is behind in Math, English, American History, Chemistry, and it's only the third week we've been back.

Max doesn't do too much outdoor soccer or tennis. It's too hot. He'd be better in France for this.

October 11, 2007

Atlanta, Grade 4

Ali took a taxi to Sarasota-Bradenton airport this morning at 6 a.m. with Lance.

Once in Atlanta, she won her first two rounds with a good showing in singles. She then lost with Emilia in doubles, first round. Although they are both lefties, their results leave a lot to be desired, and I don't surmise they'll remain together long as a doubles team.

Tulsa, Oklahoma: Grade 1

She lost 1st round singles 7-5, 5-7, 3-6 to Sara L, a good 1992 born Serb in Jose's group.

---

[61] Looking at this schedule now, with hindsight, I can see why she wanted to be on MSN. This was a killer schedule!

Today, I was stopped by Percy, who congratulated me on this loss! Left unsaid was that he considered his charge (Percy gave expensive private lessons to Sara L) to be so much better than Ali, who, he suggested sarcastically, must have been playing out of her mind to even get so close.

I wasn't so happy about it.

I told him that Ali got hooked on match point in the second set, but he said it was just one point and added that even though it was a match point and a "nasty cheat" … he made it clear that this "nasty cheat" was just Ali's uninformed and partial read on Sara's call. I responded, "partial-schmartial." Ali had assured us that her ball was very much in but was *called* out—it still wasn't an excuse for not winning in the third set. Then he softened this statement by saying Ali had really improved. The fact she hadn't won the third set was hard for me to digest—probably even harder for Ali—but unfortunately, tennis is cruel and unfortunately, he was right.

That being said, even she admitted she played very well.

Getting her homework done still presents a lot of problems for her, and she's crying out for help.

October 16, Tuesday

Montreal, Canada, Grade 3 ITF

It was great getting back to Montreal after so much time away. My first fourteen years—aside from a brief period in New York—were spent here in Westmount, the English part of Montreal.

And it was Westmount as I always remembered it—in the fall, with the hockey season just starting and brown leaves all over the ground. These had fallen from the beloved maple trees, the leaf of which is the symbol of Canada and is found on their red and white flag. As a boy, when the breeze picked up, I would race through the leaves just for the pleasure of feeling the cold wind on my face.

Back in the present, there was an arctic chill in the air, especially in the late afternoon. I gazed out over the grassy area next to the Rogers Cup stadium and realized that in about three weeks from now, the place would be completely covered in snow.

Ali is playing much better. Her doubles game has really improved. She returns and gets to net. She also serves and gets to net (sometimes too much).

Coach Tiffany D told her she must choose her times more carefully when approaching the net.

I'm amazed by the level of tennis I'm seeing. These kids seem to improve exponentially almost every day. They are hitting with incredible power and accuracy.

Ali was passed at net three times by rocket returns from their opponents, even off very good serves by her partner, the left-handed Emilia. Of the two, Ali was generally the more combative and stronger at the beginning and at the end, even saving one match point against them in their doubles first-round match. However, Emilia was the more consistent overall and held down the fort throughout this encounter which they lost 6-3, 6-4.

Their opponents, two French Canadians from Montreal—one of whom Ali barely beat in the first round—were even more impressive as they served and returned with great consistency. In addition, the Canadians consistently served first serves to our girls' backhands.

I still don't understand why the USTA and Canadian Tennis Federation don't umpire these matches using local kids who, themselves, could then be further patrolled by roaming "super" umpires. It would make the game much fairer and would really promote tennis.[62]

Final Results: Ali scraped by in her first-round singles 2-6, 6-4, 7- 6 (8-6) in the third set tiebreaker. This little Canadian was good: she'd regularly hit winners off Ali's first serves. Ali's first serve percentage was very good as well. In the second set, however, Ali's percentage dropped off a bit, but she was more combative.

In the third set, she led 3-0 and 5-3 after impressive runs in spite of a failing first-serve percentage. She also led in the tie-break except when she went behind 4-3 after a 3-1 lead. She finally won after squandering one match point at 6-5.

Win or lose, these matches are real character builders.

My notes on Montreal (to Lance L):

Singles: First-serve percentage: 70% - 75% - 55% in sets 1, 2 and 3, respectively. Ali still lost the first set 2-6 with 70% of her first balls in. Why?

---

[62] I later wrote a note to the USTA detailing my plan but, as usual, was completely ignored.

In the first two sets, her balls lacked power and height over the net. Her returns were not into her opponent's body or backhand but to her strength: her forehand. The French Canadian hit a lot of winners because Ali's serves didn't have enough kick.

In the third set, Ali fought hard to win.

Doubles: Ali was stronger at the beginning and end of the match. Emilia was more consistent and lucid throughout.

Ali is still too tough on herself.

Emilia is great when taking the ball early.

They're much more aggressive together now and happened to play a great team.

We left for Toronto four days later but not before dining with old friends and hiring a taxi to re-visit my old haunts, the house where I grew up, and my all-English boys' school, Lower Canada College in N.D.G.[63]

October 20, 2007

Toronto, Ontario, Canada, Grade 4 ITF

---

[63] Notre Dame de Grace, a predominantly French-Canadian district in Montreal.

Toronto: We stayed with old Toronto friend Ernie J. It was fantastic talking with him again. He lived in a brownstone walk-up in Rosedale, an area very similar to Westmount. Even though I had only been to Rosedale once when I was an exchange research assistant thirty-two years earlier at the University of Toronto, I felt I had never left the Westmount of my youth. In fact, Kingston-upon-Thames, England, Westmount, and Rosedale, Canada were clumped together in my memory: Myriad ivy-covered walk-ups, creamy white faces, English voices, and autumn leaves.

For Ali, however, her results were two first-round losses in both singles and doubles.

She also did not do any homework until Friday morning. Therefore, hours and hours of potential homework were left undone. She had all of Thursday night and Friday morning to get her assignments done, but instead, she is now getting further and further behind.

She's talking about leaving the online program and going back to her brick-and-mortar school, but Fran doubts the real motives behind this decision.

Is this to get together with boyfriend N?

As for this particular boyfriend, I have a little story to tell:

The young man in question is an eighteen-year-old from the Dominican Republic, enrolled in IMG for tennis and Bradenton Prep for school. One night, we gave Ali a nine o'clock curfew. She had gone to see him around eight and had not returned by 9:15, at which point I went to the Clubhouse Pool Area to find her. Apparently, that's where all the teenagers liked to hang out at night. I saw them sitting upon a bench near the hot tub, but when she saw me, she slinked off as if she had never been sitting there in the first place.

As for him, he was wearing his visor cap on sideways and looking straight ahead at the pool. That is, his visor was looking at me, but his face wasn't. I went over to him, stood there, and just stared at him. After about two minutes, I barked,

"You Neo?" He didn't look at me but nodded slowly, his visor beak doing the nodding. "Where's Ali?" The visor beak moved in the direction Ali had slunk off to. By this time, I wanted to punch the guy, but he said nothing and just stared straight ahead:

"You understand, I told her to be back at 9—it's now 9:30—she's got to get up early, she can't just while away time here talking to you at this pool, don't you have homework to do, the two of you, what are you doing hanging out here on a school night, not to speak of the heavy tennis schedule the two of you have, and what do you think I look like when I ask her to be back on time, she isn't, and just the two of you sitting here, I have no authority over her, she's not even fifteen and you, you're older, at least you have some say with her, you could have sent her home earlier so I wouldn't have had to come out here and waste my time, waste my time, do you hear me, is this important for you—whether I waste my time or not, don't you have any respect?!—so that's it, you hear? She's not coming out here again!!?"

I said this all-in-one breath, barking at him at the end.

With that, the visor beak nodded. He turned his head and glanced at me briefly, and then returned his gaze to the water.

I walked off. He had never spoken.

Later on, word went around campus that he had never been so scared of anyone in his entire life, and from this moment on, I had a new nickname that everyone seemed to know, "El Loco."[64]

---

[64] "El Loco"' means "the crazy guy."

November 2, 2007

I'm getting a little bit fed up with Ali, who does not cease to irritate me. After my run-in with Neo, I stopped her from going out on weeknights. I said she was only allowed three hours per week at a movie on Saturday night. Not one hour per day hanging out anymore. How much of this is possible to control will prove quite difficult.

Our closeness with the Ss has dissipated. She shows absolutely no interest in Ali anymore, e.g., Ali was playing Nicole B and losing badly, but Carling S was totally involved in watching her son. I suppose we shouldn't place too much hope in someone who not only charges us $120/hour for a series of lessons but who also jacks up her price to $150/hour if Ali needs the "odd" lesson.

It gets me so mad that I cannot get $80 an hour for Accent Reduction lessons when tutors at Bollettieri make that and much more. On the other hand, excellent teachers like math instructor Paul VS and Spanish tutor Mrs. S at Bradenton Prep only make $35 for extra tutoring.

Whatever he makes as a teacher, PVS did say Ali was doing better.

As for little brother Max, his school results are excellent, and his soccer and martial arts are coming along, too.

However, tennis is not for him yet. I was hoping that he'd love to hit the ball, but this doesn't seem to be the case.

I watched Ali yesterday with Jose L. She played badly right from the get-go, swiping at the court with her racquet and demonstrating bad behavior generally. She's very confrontational now, and anything I say, she holds against me. On the eve of 15, she seems very far from where I want her to go.

What does she want for herself?

This is hard to figure out. I just had a chat with one of the Bollettieri Dads. (He grounded his daughter for two months because she was horsing about with an Italian and indulging in "conduct unbecoming a lady.")

November 12, 2007

I just discovered a $545 phone bill for Ali's cell. Two calls on a Saturday night from Burlington, Ontario to Bradenton cost $45.

Total roaming charges for Ali's number are $491. I suppose it's normal, but since the calls were made to the IMG main number, then forwarded to his room, it's a bit much. I have no desire to see Ali celebrate her fifteenth birthday in two days. I don't want to be a part of it, and I certainly don't want to drive her and her friends to Gio's to celebrate it. I resent the fact we even bought her another digital camera to make up for the one she lost last summer (or was it stolen?).

Gabriele M put it very succinctly: once a kid gets into the ATP or WTA, she starts at number 1500 and basically tries to claw her way into the top thirty where she'll be able to make a decent living playing tennis.

This is the reality where they all stand.

Now, I was thinking top thirty, but maybe it's more reasonable to think top 100. As of this year, 2011, the break-even point between making a meager living and paying one's expenses is about 119 in the world for both men and women.

I wrote Lance an e-mail detailing what Ali still needs to do to become a top player:

1) She needs an overhead, especially when running back to hit a smash off her back foot (mainly, she needs to learn to run back).

2) She needs a normal, classic volley, including a stop volley.

3) She needs to start hitting high over the net—especially this—whenever she's pulled wide, she hits a low drive to see if it'll be a winner.[65] She will never get anywhere unless she stops doing this.

4) Gianluigi Q, a lefty and only eleven years old,[66] hits high balls every time he is in trouble. Why can't she do that?

5) She has to play a lot of practice matches where she is not penalized for trying things, i.e., for going to net and trying shots and blowing them and trying again.

6) She has to understand the geometry of the court. e.g., she can't continue to serve to opponents' strengths or hit hard, low shallow balls up the middle and not get blown away (from their returns) down one of the wings.

7) I have tried to sit down with her and explain court geometry, but right now, in late 2007, I'm barking up the wrong tree: she just does not want to listen to me. Maybe Lance will be able to get through to her?

December 2, 2007

---

[65] For every winner she hits, she hits two losers
[66] Now 15, Q is 82 ITF juniors in March 2011

The Tennis Bubble

Eddie Herr

I saw Emmanuel P from France, but there was no time to talk. One of us is always in a rush.

His team was down for breakfast, ready to go at 6 a.m. for the Eddie Herr.

Ali lost 6/4, 6/4 to a very beatable Belarusian in the first-round 16s. This girl was good and took a lot of time serving. In contrast, Ali served quickly and made eight double faults in two sets.

Ali makes two to three unforced errors per game. She needs height over the net on her shots. This is what we're talking about. I'm going to write this all down in a long e-mail letter to Lance.

Christmas, 2007

France

Ali played three times with Benji B, a friend of mine I used to play with and who has a men's ranking similar to Ali's women's ranking in France. She won twice, lost once.

She also trained very well with Thierry C, a real nice guy who has become a regular partner of hers. Forty-eight years old, Thierry plays like a young buck and has a similar French ranking to Ali's.

She also played and lost to another friend of mine, Antoine C, 6/1, 6/1. Antoine has a similar ranking to Benji and Thierry, but Antoine rarely makes a mistake.

Ali didn't play any tournaments in France, but she did play well.

December 23, 2007

In France, I wrote an e-mail to Lance detailing all the issues I have brought up here.

Upon receipt of my e-mail, Lance did not write back to me but apparently told Ali over the phone: "I give up. Your dad thinks he knows more about tennis than I do."

My answer is I always let the coaches have their say. In addition, I have no influence over her at all. In spite of what I've written here, I say, "Let the coaches deal with her tennis." But are they dealing with it properly?

I told Lance that after 16 ITFs in a year and a half, Ali—at #600 in the juniors—should have been doing a lot better than she was, especially with her talent. Essentially, she was playing back and playing scared—or brain dead—and always, always, to the opponent's strength. I also told him that Ali rarely played with a strategic game plan and that—like it or not—there was little "control, hurt, and finish."

"We want Ali to stand out from the pack but will she," I asked rhetorically. "Is she a leader?"

I told Lance that I was concerned that most of the Bollettieri kids—aside from a tiny few—were doing so poorly in the big junior tournaments.

Notwithstanding my perception that IMG-Bollettieri is a money-grubbing place profiting off kids and their dreams—a place in which taking good care of them comes secondary—I told Lance that we wanted the best tennis instruction for our daughter that money could buy. In addition to this, Ali will also have to work weekly on her attitude with Angus.

Lance feels that Ali needs to do small tournaments to learn how to win, whereas we, the parents, feel Ali needs to do ITFs and run forwards on the court and not backward ... both in tennis and in life.

Florida

Back in Florida, Sly B is her new primary coach. He makes her work hard and does it with style. Right now, she's putting out in intensity which is really what he wants from her. She needs to be intense in her practices. We'll see where this leads us, but I remain very positive.

Bollettieri Grand Prix[67] Tournament - Jan. 2008

---

[67] Internal Grand Prix and related tournaments are organized regularly at the NBTA throughout the year.

Ali won her first three matches: Gaia 6/2, 6/4 - Perry A 6/2, 6/2 - Dina S 7/5, 6/7, 7/5. Hallelujah! This last match showed three tough sets with a tough score line against a no-nonsense Russian. This was a very hard match which the old Ali could easily have lost!

February 6, 2008

Clearwater, Florida

I've been waiting here at Clearwater all morning.

Ali's opponent didn't show up for her morning match, and it would have been a waste of time and money to return to Bradenton, only to come right back again a couple of hours later for Ali's afternoon match. As it turned out, the girl was forty-five minutes late.

Ali has no computer, no books to read but is very happy chewing the fat with her friends Juliana M and Nicole B. Two other kids are reading and studying, but she is socializing. Frankly, it's my fault for not bringing something for both of us to do.

Is it good for her to waste so much time, and what can I do about it? In addition, she misses out on school as well as training with Sly and the group and Lance: a bit silly, the whole thing ... Sometimes I ask myself, "Do I need this great Florida weather all the time?"

After winning the morning match by default, she lost this second match 1 and 0.

Here are my notes: 1st set: Not ready to play. Choice of side: She chooses to serve even though she's been losing a lot of her service games. She wins her first service game, and in the second game, she has two breakpoints on the other girl's serve. Suddenly, she stops running and keeps going back—is she sleepwalking? Tired? Where is the "go-go-go!?"

Suddenly, she starts playing to the girl's strength, her forehand. She plays too weak, too low, and starts doing all the running. She loses this return game and then her next service game at love. She doesn't try. It's as if she's standing there.

Second set: Now she complains her strings are too loose.[68] I'm her stringer at this point and what is implied is that it's my fault even though I've strung dozens of racquets with no complaints). More games go by at love.

Beneath my calm exterior, I'm questioning everything.

Are you waiting for your opponent to make a mistake, I ask Ali within myself? Are you brain dead? Why aren't you using spin? Why do you retreat back on your side after every shot? *I'm not criticizing you if you make a mistake trying to do something going forward, girl. But I don't understand wanting to retreat two meters behind the baseline and "taking it" from the opposition!*

February 11, 2008

Goodbye, Lance, hello Sly!

---

[68] Strings lose 8 to 10% of their tension within a few hours of stringing.

She is training well with Sly—we're not dealing with Lance as much now—but she still hasn't learned to win like she can. She is still in the midst of adolescence: Boys, girlfriends who aren't, teenage stuff ... To me, this is the main issue—aka problem—and once it and a commitment to hard physical work is shown, she will really go somewhere, if she wants, which is a big "if." To be blunt, everything's still up in the air.

The old argument—that since a kid doesn't really know what he wants, one has to expose said kid to certain beneficial influences which should take root—is no longer holding water. She's now fifteen, has been playing tennis since the age of five, and if she doesn't "get it" this year, I fear she never will. We really can't tell her what she's capable of. She has to show us what she's got, and quite frankly, she has only done so in fits and starts.

February 24, 2008

We're still trying to figure out what to do for the next school year. If she doesn't go to Bollettieri, she can still go on with Sly and do her studies online—from Florida. Or she can forget Sly, go to France with a private coach and also continue her studies online.

She played a first-round yesterday in a local super series and would have been blown out or had a tough match two and a half years ago when she arrived here. Now Ali runs through these easily, winning 6-1, 6-0 with only one game lost due to inattention. In other words, Ali has come a long way. Sly has made a big difference, really focusing on her net game and having her come forward.

Fifteen-year-old Giacomo M is going to Texas to play a future. Playing ATP futures at fifteen is pretty impressive for someone so young.

February 27, 2008

Ali lost her semi-final to a Ukrainian 1-6, 6-4, 2-6. This was very disappointing in that the Ukrainian was only 12 years old. Ali had no energy. Again, this morning, she should have been on the court at 6:30 a.m. but did not get up.

She needs a "physical trainer" to get her going on her physical training. I do what I can when she allows me to, but she rarely lets me help her. Whenever I speak, I'm drowned out by excuses, loud noises, silence, or interruptions. Oh well, it'll be her loss.

She's been in Lance's strategy zone program now for three years but uses little strategy when she plays. She still serves the great majority of her serves to the righties'[69] strengths, i.e., usually the forehand. This is clearly not acceptable.

March 7, 2008

Costa Rica, Grade 4

Ali went with Coach Tiffany and Emilia to Costa Rica and won her first round against an unknown Mexican

---

[69] Nine out of ten tennis players play right-handed.

6-3, 6-0. However, she lost in the second round against Dina G, a girl she sometimes plays in Bollettieri by the score of 6-4, 3-6, 4-6. In this match, she led in all three sets, including 3/1 in the second, where she lost five games in a row. Why?

Then again, she led 4/3, 40-30 in the third when the girl made a great shot. That was only one point, but after Ali lost that point, she was deflated, lost two quick points to lose the game, and then went away, losing the next two games and match in quick succession.

Back in Bollettieri, at first, she neither wanted to practice nor play in this afternoon's Grand Prix tournament but relented and is going to play it after all. Afterward, she'll start up with Sly again.

Preparing to take the SAT language tests in French and Italian one day, she continues to study with Mme. S on her French and with her mother on her Italian.

March 14, 2008

I have no idea what is going on. My wife spends hours with Ali discussing her friends, My Space, YouTube, and everything else related to being a teenager.

I don't. I have little patience for it.

As Max runs into our bed every night, I suggested exchanging our big king-size bed for three Goldilocks beds in our bedroom: Papa bear, Mama bear, and little Baby bear Max beds.

I really feel estranged from my daughter. How long will this go on?

As for tournaments, everything is up in the air. Will Ali go off for a summer Caribbean tour or what? Ali will never just stay with Emily and Lance's wife, Anne M, in the States. But will Tiffany come to France and stay with us, and will Lance even let her? If Tiffany is with her boyfriend, I suppose we could let them stay over there. And that would feel a little strange, but I could get over it.

Ali's studying hard now, and tennis now takes second place to everything social, but I guess that's just the way life is. I speak my mind, but no one listens.

March 30, 2008

It's been thirty-eight years since my father died—on a tennis court. He threw the ball up to serve and dropped dead from a massive stroke or a brain clot—we never found out. Ali had asked me a few weeks back how I had reacted at the time he died, and I told her:

"I didn't cry. I got angry with everybody. I worried about how I would have to deal with telling everybody about it, and then, about six months later, I imagined him lying in the ground."

She thought I was weird.

Junior ITFs

Trinidad

Ali and her partner Marie-Frederique B, a Canadian from Montreal, went to the finals in doubles!

Ali also won three rounds in singles, including 6-1 in the third set against Marie-Frederique.[70] After losing in singles, Marie-Frederique pulled out just before playing the doubles finals and left Ali without a partner. According to M-F's coach, she had to "get back to" Montreal.

What would have happened had she beaten Ali in singles? I'm sure M-F B would have found the money and a way to change her flight plans, and they would have played their final doubles together.

---

[70] According to the sports clipping in the local paper, Ali was currently #522 and M-F B, #466 ITF.

This happens a lot—people pulling out once they've lost in singles—but remember that's what Ali had to do to her doubles partner in Mobile, Alabama for the 14s National when she had to return to Bollettieri to play the Eddie Herr in November 2006. In tennis, and especially in tennis, what goes around comes around!

April 2008

Barbados

Another West Indian island, but not the same result:

Ali said she didn't play very well, but I don't remember the details. The irony is that she and her team stayed in a hotel in St. Lawrence Gap that was built in the same place as a bed and breakfast I used to stay at as a young boy during the winter.

The End of the Road with Lance

On April 4, 2008, Fran and I received this e-mail from Lance. "I need to see you and Francesca ASAP. Ali is out of control, and Tiffany doesn't trust her. She broke the rules—again. That's three times in one week. She was caught in another person's room—it turned out to be a girl's—at 11:30 p.m. after Tiffany put the kids in their room at 10 p.m. I am almost certain that I won't send Tiffany with Ali to Morocco after this experience."

We tried to get together with Lance immediately, but as it turned out, we didn't get in to see him until ten days later. We talked it over and decided we would end the whole relationship.

Essentially, Ali had given up on him but so had we. Over the last three years, we had spent about $20,000/year just for him while it was really Guillermo, Carling, Julian, and Sly who were doing the most for her.

They had actually been professional tennis players, but he hadn't.

However, I liked the fact that he spent a lot of time talking about the positive aspects of Ali's tennis, how he wanted to bring her up the tennis ladder, and how he really believed in her. He talked about things that interested me, her bad attitude, and how her dismissive attitude was not conducive to playing good tennis. He was also very frank about how she was being led around by the "in-crowd"—the Latin connection—and he was right.

He was particularly annoyed that in the fall of 2007, he had Ali believing in him and his program. But then the "in-crowd"—in Ali's case, the Latin Connection—had taken over and had seized full control of Ali's brain. Culturally, he was limited in dealing with Ali, but he was completely right about her being out of control.

Unfortunately, within his group of students, Lance was surrounded by a bunch of low achievers. He would teach strategy, but these kids hadn't even mastered the fundamentals and the tools they should have learned properly at Bollettieri.[71]

---

[71] God knows that these fundamentals were taught over and over again. It just goes to show that it is not what is taught but what is retained that is the answer and this is why so many are called and so few are chosen.

Financial Fact

In 2007-8, Ali's last year at Bollettieri, the tuition was $26,631, which was then increased to $32,100, a difference of 21% or $5469 for the upcoming 2008-9 academic year! This huge price increase from one season to the next played a significant part in our not enrolling her for the next year. It was an insult to our intelligence how we and all the other student athletes and their families were being played for suckers, especially when she was hardly using the Academy and having to go off campus all the time for extra lessons.

Ali is still acquiring the fundamentals: The courage to go to net, the courage to hit an overhead or volley to put away the point. Lance's concept of tennis—control, hurt, and finish—is dead on. Unfortunately, we both didn't understand that she needed her life to be simple and not driven solely by a future sports ranking, that she needed to be able to hang out with her friends as well as play tennis and study.[72]

Despite her talent, Ali continues to underachieve. In fact, everyone says she has talent, but the reality is she melts down and goes away on a tennis court. In the spring of 2008, I would rather describe her very objectively in the following way:

She has great speed, good technique, a wonderful overhead (which she rarely uses), a great backhand, a lethal forehand, and a fabulous serve she never hits out on.

But her emotional "heart" is weak.

---

[72] Mind you, had Ali established a winning record and/or dramatically improved her tennis, she might not have been so attracted by this alternative social life. Does winning solve all problems? No, but it helps!

She has tremendous range—which she uses off the court to significant dramatic effect—but she still doesn't channel her rage into her tennis.

Against Sara L two weeks ago, Ali went down 1 and 3 because she was tired. She had simply gone to bed too late.

She continues to spend a lot of her free time doing MSN. She is behind in her sophomore year despite a group of teachers and parents looking out for her. Maybe she'll finish her English and Math this summer. Maybe not.

Anthony, her physical trainer, has had a good effect on her, but why was she puffing in her match against Sara? Why did she not call the four obvious cheating calls against her? Does she care? In a few hours, she'll be playing Tristan in an Academy internal tournament. I fear the worst simply because Tristan is so consistent. But if Ali plays her game, maybe she can do it.

John E[73] called and wants to play with Ali. Obviously, he's trying to recruit her to his academy, but we're happy with what we've got with Sly and Anthony. And I've arranged for a final goodbye lesson with Julian.

Intramural tournament results

---

[73] John E and Johan K were a top South African 1980s doubles team and both excellent singles players in their own right. Only about 5'8", Johan K went as high as number 7 in the world. John and Johan both started an Academy in Longboat Key but then went their separate ways in the Tampa Bay area.

Match 1: Ali loses to Sara S 6-0, 3-6, 2-6. Ali was winning comfortably 6-0, 3-0 when Mother Dana made a scene—in *English* and not in Serbian (she always talks to her daughter in Serbian) so we spectators would all understand—then went away, and Ali only got two games after that, losing 8 in a row at one point.

Match 2: Ali loses to Tristan D, 6-1, 6-1.

Taking Match 2 first, Ali was nowhere to be found, making error after error and playing with no confidence. I almost felt sorry for her that she was crushed so badly.

Concerning Match 1, I talked to Mama Dana afterward. She apologized over and over to all of us and even to Nick Bollettieri for the way she interfered in the Ali-Sara match.

But it was too late since the damage had already been done.

Nick didn't see it this way, however, because in the long run, it's not about who wins what but rather how one's character is formed. In this case, Sara S received a good kick in the proverbial behind and won the match. Ali, on the other hand, was easily distracted and intimidated and somehow made to feel guilty for playing good tennis. As a result, she lost the match.

Both learned from their shared experience.

Nick also agreed with her that Dana should go nuts if Sara was messing about, even if that meant disrupting and changing the match's whole outcome—Sara calling her boyfriend during changeovers, not trying hard enough, not concentrating while serving, not grunting while hitting, etc. Mind you, Ali was making it difficult for her as she was hitting out on everything and succeeding.

I told the mother I thought she should stay quiet, sit down and not disrupt her daughter, and if she did have to disrupt her, she should do it discreetly in the Serbian language. Mile, the father (who was not watching), agreed with me, saying that Sara played better when Dana was not there. Dana told me that she couldn't stand to watch her daughter play like that. I told her I felt her pain but that I had had to endure matches like that day after day (Ali vs. Sara L, Ali vs. Sara S, Ali vs. Tristan D, and unfortunately, the list goes on) with my daughter.

"You shouldn't accept that," she responded. "You should speak up and make a scandal, just like I did. You shouldn't put up with that."

"But I thought you were sorry?" I responded.

"I am," she said, "for you, but personally, I couldn't take it anymore. I didn't care if Sara won or lost. I just wanted her to play well, so I left!"

I pointed out that Dana had established a reputation of behaving like this, and she wanted to know who had told me that. She wanted specifics of matches and dates and times, but I told her it was general knowledge and refused to reveal my sources. She told me she was a "pro-active" mother and that I should be a "pro-active" father and not tolerate it when my child played like a loser. I told her that I always let my daughter know when she played like a schlemiel, and I even raised my voice as well, but it was usually about behavioral issues like when she threw her racquet. She told me that the Ss were a tennis family, and everything revolved around their daughters' tennis. I told her "ditto" and let her know in no uncertain terms that if Ali were ever to play one of their daughters and Dana created a similar scene, I would call the umpire immediately and make a much bigger scene.

We parted as "wary" friends. No one gave in to the other, but the fact remains that my daughter lost because she was thrown off her game by outside pressure.

So much the worse for her.

Somewhere around this time, I wrote Ali a long e-mail with a copy to Fran. In it, I took Ali apart for being too immature and a crowd-pleaser rather than a leader. I criticized her for not cleaning up after herself in the morning, procrastinating in her studies, and generally not being serious enough about her tennis. I asked her rhetorically,

"Do you practice to win, or do you practice to practice during a match? What I was most concerned about in your match against Tristan was how she completely cleaned your clock, and you sat back and let her do it as you appeared to worry about your wayward forehand.

"Here is a girl a year and a half younger than you—one you used to beat—who outworked, outthought, outhustled, and completely outplayed you.

"I even felt bad for you because it looked like you were trying, and you were very frustrated. From the beginning, there was no smile, just a pained look on your face—like someone about to mess their pants with no place to go. There was no joy or seriousness in trying to solve a problem: how to beat Tristan.

"Tennis is like a game of chess but much simpler even though more tiring physically. The right attitude to have is "how do I beat her"? Let's *try* this plan, or that plan, etc.

"What was your plan? To worry about your forehand when that is something you do in practice, not in matches? Or to experiment with different shots to find out which one would bother her? How about thinking move my butt, hit forehands to her backhand, get the short reply, and put it away? How about looping a heavy topspin ball to her backhand and moving to the net once in a while? Or concentrating so hard on putting the ball in the court—to one side or the other obviously—that you don't make the error after the second or third shot—which is, unfortunately, the norm for you? Do you think that helps your confidence or your desire to play—and believe me, as a former player, I feel for you—to play this way?

"Remember, when you play, you play to win. You keep the ball in play, establish your game plan—attack her serve, hit to the forehand or backhand as the case may be—and you execute. When you practice, you practice hard with a specific goal in mind because if you don't, you'll never get the results on the court and in matches."

Then, in big letters, I wrote,

"It works this way: You practice hard to play well, and when you play well, you get results, and when you get results, you feel better, which makes you practice harder, and then you play better, and then your results are even better which makes you feel even happier? Capisce?"

Then I ended my e-mail on this note and in big letters: "Basically, are you going to follow the crowd and be a pleaser and follower, or are you going to do your own thing and be a leader?"

To this day, I don't know if she even read this e-mail.

Did she delete it without reading it? Is it Spam?

Such is our communication.

Future Directions

At this point in early May of 2008, we—as well as Ali, and this is an important distinction—were seriously considering Plan B[74]: sending Ali to college so she could play on a tennis team and earn a four-year athletic scholarship. Yes, she wanted to both go to college—one day—as well as play tennis.

But she wasn't entirely sure.

So we had to make a contingency Plan A+ for college. For this, we were going to use the College Source program at Bollettieri. This organization would help Ali prepare for her SAT entry exam and would introduce her to coaches for the future.

In the meantime, she would continue to work on Plan A, which was a career in professional tennis.

---

[74] There are certain people who stigmatize the use of this term "Plan B" as in "everyone has to have a Plan B." The feeling is, "if you have to have a Plan B, then you don't have enough of a Plan A." Real champions don't have a Plan B. They roar straight ahead to Plan A. Furthermore, these people feel that admitting the existence of a Plan B is tantamount to being a loser. My feeling is that even the number 1 men and women's players in the world didn't spend their whole day playing tennis on their way up and they all needed some career after the age of thirty so maybe we need to call Plan B, *Plan A+*.

The Tennis Bubble

Alessandra hitting an inside-out forehand winner

Alex 2011 USF Tennis

Alex 2011 USF Tennis

The Tennis Bubble

Alex Match Stats 2009-10

Ali and Nicola in Naples, Florida: 2006

Alessandra in Naples, Florida tourney

The Tennis Bubble

Angry Alessandra at another tournament
4-1-2006

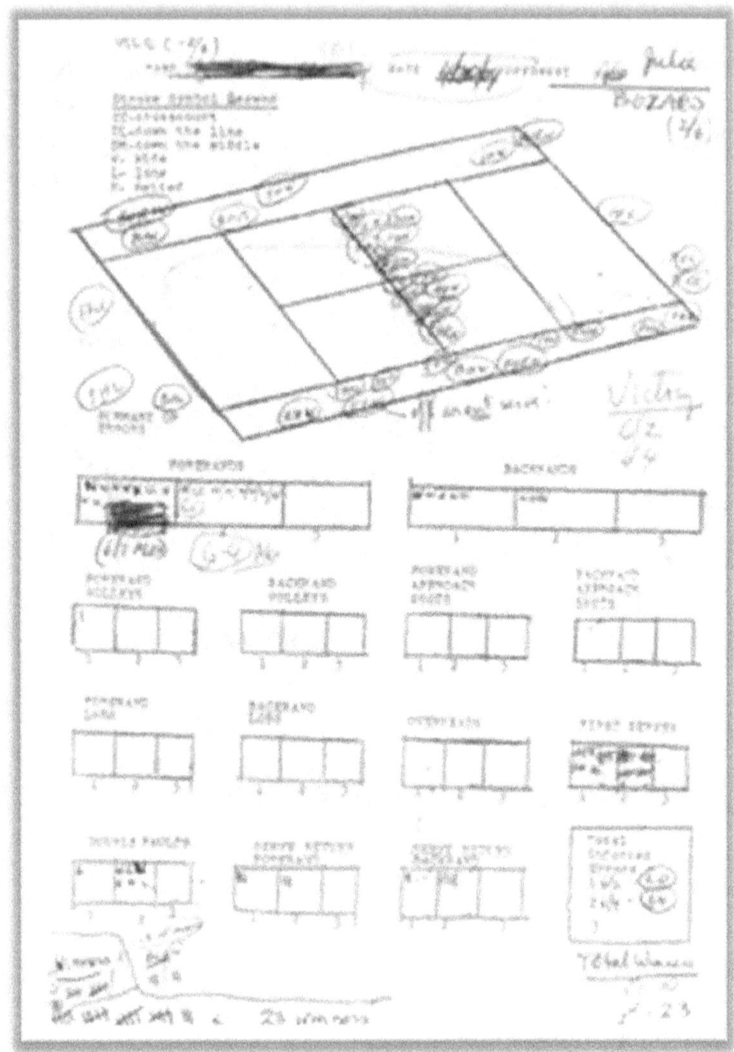

Ball placement diagram:
Victory 6-2 6-4 against "2-6" ranked
Julie Bezard, May 1, 2009

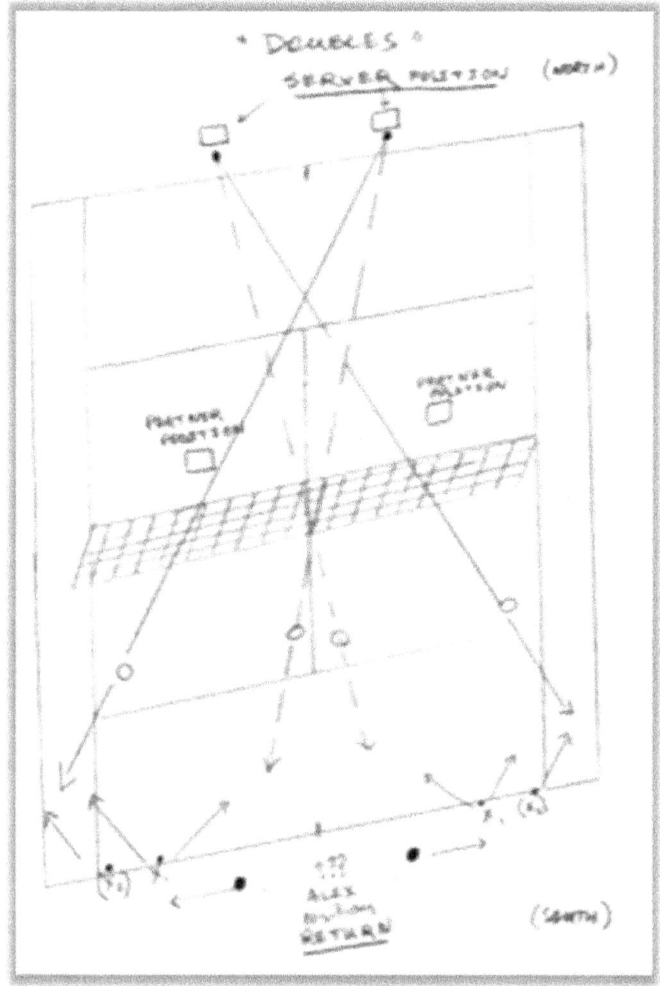

Doubles Diagram

The Tennis Bubble

Match Stats Bonte-Zowczak
5-6-2009

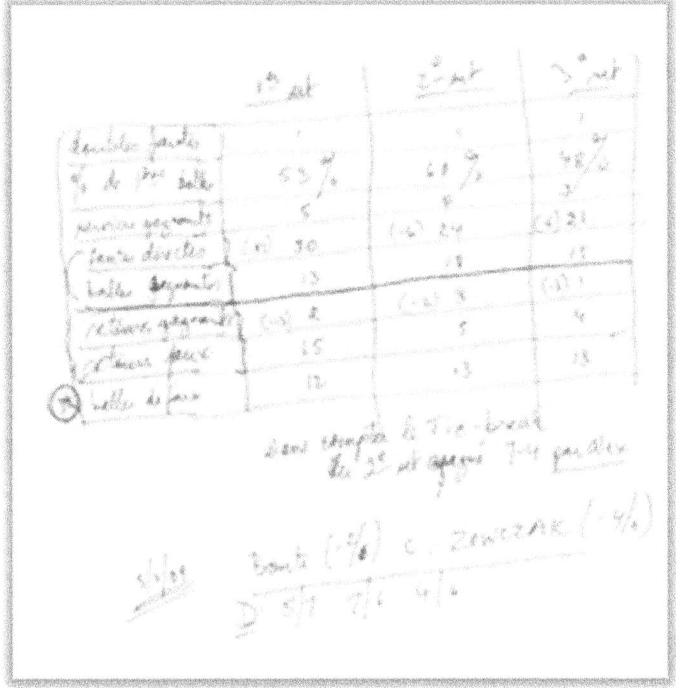

Match Summary Bonte-Zowczak
5-6-2009

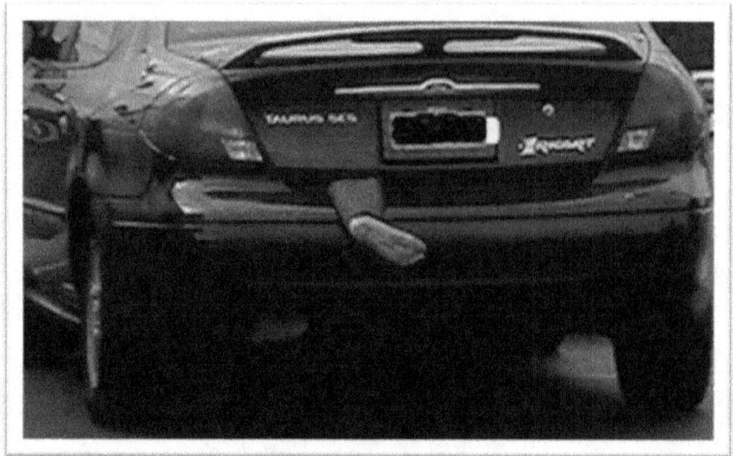

Pre-Halloween in Cincinnati
Oct. 23, 2006

The Tennis Bubble

**The Cincinnati National Junior Indoor Tournament
Oct. 2006**

The Tennis Bubble

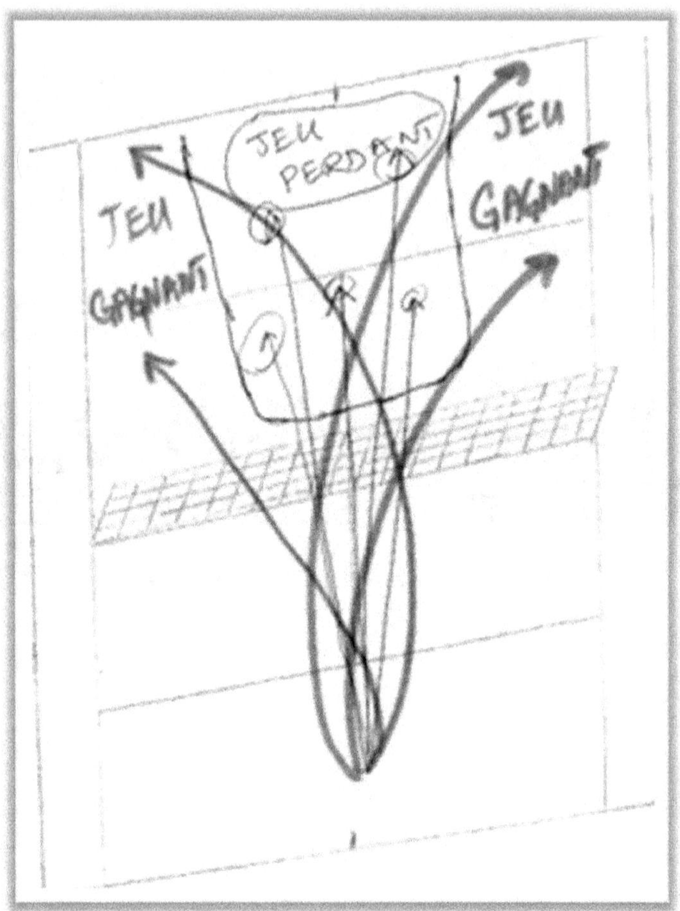

U-Zone on Tennis Court

CHAPTER 5:

Post-Bollettieri

In the spring of 2008, we left Bradenton to spend the summer in France and Italy. I stayed at home in France with Max while Francesca and Ali immediately went to Morocco for a series of four ITF $10,000 tournaments in the cities of Rabat and Casablanca.

I thought back over her three years at Bollettieri. In French terms, she had gone from 15/2 in 2005 to 0 in 2008, increasing seven French ranking levels. After just one year in Bollettieri, Ali was already playing at a 2/6 French level—maybe higher—a very high level indeed.

Christmas 2006 had been very revealing.

She had pulled off a Count-of-Monte-Cristo feat by knocking off all her old adversaries, and this showed us that maybe Ali was going to be able to fly on her own tennis-wise after all.

But then her results between 2006 and 2008 had been very up and down. She had played well at times and had usually worked very hard at her tennis, but her match results were not reflecting this fact.

Then came the spring of 2008. She had been working harder than ever, playing a lot of tough, physical tennis off-campus with Sly B. and Anthony B. Still, she wasn't getting the results worthy of her efforts. Especially at the Academy. Or in any important tournament, for that matter.

Then came Morocco.

Morocco was a revelation for us. Thought to be a place where one could pick up many easy ITF points, Morocco 2008 was quite the opposite. Since everyone and his mother or father had the same idea of scooping up easy ITF points in far-away places, the best players all converged on out-of-the-way Morocco, making this particular series of tournaments incredibly difficult. Ali rose to the challenge and beat two top, world-ranked juniors—Emi M and Camille S—in qualifying! This was all the more gratifying in that Ali had lost 0 and 1 against Emi M in her first ITF the year before!

After a month with Ali in Morocco, Francesca was convinced that Ali needed a personal tennis coach. Francesca thought that it wasn't very professional—a girl traveling with her mother—especially since Ali was forced to compete, not only with other girls in other equally good academies but also with ones who were encouraged by their coaches.

Coach Andres M, an excellent Spanish coach of another boy, had been present throughout Ali's Morocco matches and had taken a genuine interest in her. Francesca asked him to be Ali's coach, but he traveled too much with other players and took on a full-time position in Canada.

At this point, we thought of going back to the States in the fall, dropping the Bollettieri Academy, and finding a full-time coach there who could travel with her. We wanted a woman coach for understandable reasons, but the cost was prohibitive. Because of what had happened during the spring of 2008 with Strategy Zone, Tiffany D[75]. was excluded. Ali liked Margie Z, the other coach at Strategy Zone, but she was accepted full-time at the Academy.

---

[75] Tiffany D originally wanted to live with us in France and go to tournaments with Ali. However, the chemistry between Ali and Tiffany wasn't

The Tennis Bubble

the best.

Enter Tough-talking Giorgio and Marc

I had been talking to my sister Margaret B about all this when she mentioned that she was taking tennis lessons from Guy B and that his boss, Giorgio B, a half-French, half-Argentinean entrepreneur, was looking for players to develop. He managed the "Chataigneraie" tennis club in Rueil-Malmaison, an old-time club with top-of-the-line, completely covered clay courts that served as a training ground for French Open players when they came to town.

When Giorgio heard that fifteen-year-old Ali was looking for a coach, he was all over me like a cheap suit, calling me morning and night. We brought Ali in to see him, and he talked to her like no one had ever talked to her before.

He seemed to genuinely want to take her on, but on his terms.

He arranged another meeting the next day with a French, black belt kick-boxing physical trainer called Marc, who, with his shaved head, serious manner, and tight-lipped sense of humor, was very intense.

The two of them grilled Ali for two hours, questioning her motives, her training, and everything else to do with competing in top-level tennis. I almost felt sorry for her, but I had to sit there and watch them shake her down, and I thought it was a good thing.

Long used to being coddled as a princess, Ali was intimidated. These guys essentially told her that even though she looked like a princess, she wasn't supposed to be one on the tennis court, but if she worked, if she applied herself, the world was her oyster, especially since she could really play.

They were tough on her, but they were also positive: if she had the right desire and attitude, then she could do anything. And they believed in her, perhaps more than she believed in herself. They also shared my point of view that Ali would become a professional player: in fact, why shouldn't it be she rather than someone else?

I'll repeat that: Why shouldn't she become the next top player?

This is something I've always believed, and it hooked me right away. *Why not her?* Why should it always be someone else? At last, I had found someone like myself: someone who really believed in her!

One of the first things that Giorgio B did was to have Ali play him. He was forty-five and had been a good club player. He figured that if she couldn't beat a club player easily, what future would she have as a pro?

Ali played him and barely won. Giorgio bawled her out for this in no uncertain terms and shouted that if she could win love and love, she should do so.

Then, she played him a second time and lost badly. She was told off again for lack of effort, and Marc told her he believed she really didn't want to play. Since this was like Yours Truly talking, I liked their style. They weren't going to kiss her ass. They would put her in her place, and since I couldn't do this because I was her father, I appreciated their approach.

Now Giorgio didn't want to be her coach, but he did want to be her manager. Giorgio believed in the team approach: coach, physical trainer, manager, and parents all sharing the same goal: making a professional player out of Ali. Ali already had a coach in Guillermo P-R who was pretty tough on her and someone she respected and trusted. The problem was Guillermo was two plane hours away in Sardinia, and we were in France. Also, we were still committed to going back to Florida come the fall of 2008. Since the desire was to get a full-time traveling coach, and since P-R had a tennis center and a family to attend to and couldn't travel, I had to explore other options.

Ali was fifteen—not young in tennis terms—and the time to get her game in shape was now. She was ranked 0 in France—an excellent ranking for a fifteen-year-old but only an average ranking for a future professional—and she first needed to win everything in sight at a local level before going national and international. This was a step back in thinking for all of us because Ali had been playing ITF tournaments for a year and a half already, and now we were asking her to think small again—French small—and be humble.

But the question still remained: France or Florida?

Giorgio helped us make our minds up. After having received Ali's commitment to wanting to really work on her tennis during the next three years, he asked her brutally: "well, what have your results been in ITFs?" After seventeen ITF junior tournaments—and aside from one memorable singles Grade 5 final in Dublin, a doubles win in a Grade 5 junior ITF in Guadeloupe, a doubles semi-final in a Grade 5 in Guadalajara, a first-round win in a Grade 3 junior ITF in Montreal, and a couple of other first-round wins in Grade 4s and 5s—Ali usually lost in the first round if she didn't have to qualify. She was ranked 330+ in the Junior World and would have to spend a lot of money just to play in numerous tournaments and work her way up into the top 50 Juniors. Giorgio reasoned—at least I thought he was being reasonable—why not keep Guillermo P-R, your coach in Sardinia (we were all about to go there for the summer of 2008 anyway)? I'll find a coach here who will work with you every day when you come back to France on my courts in Rueil-Malmaison. Marc will turn you into a physical phenomenon, and you'll go with your French coach every week to local and national tournaments around France? This will save you a lot of money for travel and hotels, and you'll really find out where you stand.

This sounded like a great plan. The only thing that my wife didn't like was that we were not going back to Florida with its pleasant weather. But then Max would be enrolled in the Lycée International where he would be studying three days a week in French and one day a week in English as well as benefiting from all the French medical, musical, and sports programs that befit a highly socialistic yet capitalistic country. We wouldn't have travel costs, and Ali would be pursuing her online school program from Bradenton and tennis dreams in France, the country where she grew up. I would have to go back to Florida, sell our cars, and bring back a lot of our stuff. Then, we would be able to rent our Florida condos and deal with the French house properly—by living in it.

All went very well for a while.

Ali was able to work online with us, and we were able to tutor her when needed. We went as a family to Sardinia, and she went to the finals of the Sardinian championships and a Grade 4 junior ITF. She worked out hard with Guillermo P-R, who was both her physical trainer and coach. By the fall of 2008, she was crushing girls ranked at the same level as she and pushing higher-ranked girls to three sets. Giorgio had found Isabelle G., a tough-playing but very sweet 27-year-old French coach, to work out with Ali daily. Isabelle would then step aside and let Guillermo P-R take over for two days when he came to Paris once a month to stay with us. Guillermo would make sure that Ali's technique was up to snuff and wasn't being changed by Isabelle or anyone else, for that matter.

To guarantee that Ali's technique wasn't messed with, her boyfriend, Simone,[76] would come over from Sardinia once a month to be with her and go with her to tennis tournaments. She had met Simone during the Sardinian tournament where she had gone to the finals of the women's, and he had won the men's division. Simone had worked under Guillermo P-R for five years previously and played with the same technique as Guillermo did.

As for Giorgio, he made sure she bought the Babolat equipment he had for sale, sold her balls and court time, and brought her in regularly for de-briefings and motivational harangues. Whenever Guillermo or Simone came to town, Giorgio made sure he took us all out to lunch or dinner—*at my expense.*

He made it known he was no charity operation, but he did want Ali to excel at her tennis and regularly challenged her to matches: if she didn't win easily, he told her off. He kept repeating to her—and I must say I liked his style regarding tennis—that if she couldn't beat him easily, how was she going to advance competitively against her own peers?

Ali didn't like hearing what he had to say, but I interpreted his overall message in a different way: Ali needed to take her tough, me-first, overly critical, sometimes nasty and entitled attitude *out of* her everyday life where it was *not* needed and *into* her tennis where it *was* needed.

---

[76] Pronounced "Si-<u>mown</u>-ay".

To put it in "cliché" format: One needed a big ego to win matches *on the court*. One needed to step up to the plate, do the heavy lifting, hit that extra ball, and challenge cheaters and whiners at their own game. O*n the court*. One especially needed concentration—just like a musician needs to concentrate for the entire duration of a symphony so as not to make any mistakes and still contribute his own personal interpretation to the concerto—throughout the whole course of a match.

Once the last point ended, the match was over, but during the match, Ali needed to give her all—no hurt feelings later, no "could-have, should-have, didn't" regrets down the stretch. Ali needed to feel like an entitled winner out there *during the match* and play like one.

Unfortunately, this was not to be the case. First of all, Isabelle tried to change Ali's service motion as both opponent and coach—one of the best aspects of Ali's game—right from the get-go. When Ali told us of this unwanted "teaching," I immediately intervened and told Isabelle, Giorgio, and Guillermo that I didn't want any changes to her technique.

Also, Isabelle disagreed with Guillermo's coaching and didn't want to take a back seat to him in Ali's development. Essentially, Isabelle was jealous that a fifteen-year-old girl would receive this much attention, but she never said so. Also, Isabelle was supposed to take Ali to tournaments, but she was always busy working half-time for Giorgio and never had time to take Ali herself, which meant Francesca or I would. Now, Giorgio knew we would taxi her all over the place and basically counted on this so he could work Isabelle harder at his own club and thereby pocket more money for himself from her teaching. Finally, there was the added complication of Ali only allowing her mother to ferry her about as now—at age fifteen—she didn't want my having anything to do with her tennis.

It was only a matter of time before Ali started finding "problems" with Isabelle: Essentially that she was not "simpatico" and "too French."

And there were other problems too.

Outside of tennis, Ali was not really happy studying online and took out her frustrations on anyone who happened to be around her. She found math particularly difficult, but I could tutor her, and she seemed to improve.

During the first half of 2009, Ali's tennis results remained static, and she was not able to rise above her new and improved French ranking level of -2/6. She did give me a big tennis present on my birthday at the end of February by easily winning twice in one of Giorgio's tournaments, including a great win over nemesis Pauline L who had—as previously mentioned, in cahoots with her father-coach—cheated and misbehaved during the Christmas, 2006 tournaments in the Jean Bouin/Lagardere tennis club in Paris.

The Tennis Bubble

By the early spring of 2009, we decided to part ways with Giorgio and Isabelle and had Ali go to Sardinia and work full-time with Guillermo P-R. Guillermo had been her one stable coach that she had seen every summer since 2003, and he was the one responsible for her technically sound tennis. He had shown more interest in her than any coach heretofore, even monitoring her heartbeat and helping her watch her weight and diet. He had always believed in her and was the only person who said her serve and smash were her best shots. He suggested she move into his guest house overlooking the Geovillage Tennis Center in Sardinia and live with his older daughter and sister-in-law. Ali would have to wash her own clothes, manage her homework and clean her quarters as well as eat with his family. She would have internet, and we would have to pay for her room and board as well as her tennis and physical training. She was now sixteen, old enough to take care of herself, and Guillermo thought it would be a good way for her to mature, both on and off the court.

At the time, we thought it was a good idea, too. She would gain some independence while being near her boyfriend, Simone M., who lived in nearby Olbia and taught for Guillermo.

For two months, everything went pretty well. Ali was not only training with Simone and Guillermo, but she was also practicing with Italian and South American ATP players ranked in the top 500 in the world. These were Guillermo's former students or opponents who would come to Sardinia for a few weeks to train for the European clay season.

Ali was also training very hard physically. Guillermo would have her run on the treadmill and monitored her heart rate as he pushed her to the limit. I liked him because he appeared to be very aware of physical limitations and what the body can and cannot do.

He seemed to know what he was doing. He also wasn't big on women lifting heavy weights, just light weights with numerous repetitions, to strengthen joints and muscles. Although she found it very difficult, she seemed to be satisfied at the time because we would regularly chat on Skype or the telephone, and she would tell us what great physical shape she was in.

Then, during the third week of May 2009, at the beginning of the French Open, Guillermo started behaving very strangely. Often on his cell phone and therefore not very communicative anyway with whomever he happened to be around, this time he seemed to want to avoid us, Ali's parents. He wouldn't stay with us anymore at the house. He didn't call us to talk about Ali's previous two months in Sardinia. Previously very friendly and chatty, he no longer was. Although he did obtain free passes for Ali to get into the French Open, he avoided her while hanging out with other players and coaches. She would walk the grounds alone or hang out with friends she used to know and other players.

After the tournament was over—Guillermo and Ali had not gone out once to hit even though I was paying for them to do so— and he had returned to Sardinia, even though we thought he was still in Paris. We called him to find out what was wrong. He essentially told us that he was through with the tennis center in Olbia where he worked—that they owed him a lot of money—and that he was leaving all his players as well as his wife and children to take up with a Chilean girlfriend he had met in the weight room where Ali had been training the past two months!

Ali was devastated, and even though he made it clear that his upcoming move had nothing to do with his faith in Ali as a tennis player—he was actually abandoning his whole former life and family—she was not to take it personally.

She took it personally.

Or maybe it was the fact that she was getting quite tired of tennis, and this was a convenient excuse to no longer play hard, to let herself go and do the minimum. However, I didn't think so. Whatever it was, this abandonment marked a significant break-up of Ali's tennis career, and the three of us decided it was time for Ali to see a psychologist on a regular basis …

The Tennis Bubble

The Tennis Bubble

CHAPTER 6:

Beginning of the (Tennis) End

July 8, 2009

It has been a month since the end of the French Open, and we have totally entered the world of psychology, which is all that counts for Ali now. At this time, we can't talk to her about tennis since this is such a painful subject for her.

Last week, I finally realized that Ali had grown very weary of tennis during an important tournament in Auxerre, France. Guillermo P-R's departure had really hit her hard.

In this journal entry, I feel she is at the end of the line rather than at the beginning of a tennis career, and she is only sixteen. The good news is that she has found an excellent therapist, a French woman, whom we personally happen to find very "simpatico."

I myself have been re-reading a how-to book about parenting teenagers. A bit late, you might surmise. Fundamentally, it is more of a slap in the face for us—her parents—than for her. This book appears to be saying that our "abnormal" expectations for her are the problem, not her normal expectations for herself.

All I ever wanted was for her to realize her potential. But my wish was the problem: I was usurping hers.

In other words, we should not be demanding such high achievement for our progeny. She must be the one to seek such achievement, *should she want to.*

I have to remember she's just a typical teenager trying to find her way. From my perspective, what seems to be significant for her right now is her image, fashion, and what's cool. Like for most teenagers, tennis is way down the ladder of importance.

Actually, I always suspected this but didn't want to accept it.

Over the past few months, I have witnessed time and again matches where she holds even for a while—with people she could or should beat—but then wilts in the stretch with many scores in the 6-3, 6-0 range.[77] After her last 6-2, 6-0 drubbing from a girl who was not any better than she, I realized that Ali no longer had it in her—she couldn't truly concentrate for more than a couple of games per set, i.e., *really* focus.

Recently, she has admitted that many girls at Bollettieri used to openly hope it would rain so that they wouldn't have to play each other. They were all so afraid to lose. At home, the loser would get balled out by their overly optimistic parents. On the courts at the Academy, the child would be demoted to the lower group.

Random Notes from 2009

- Most people don't want to stand out and be counted. They would rather "let things happen."

---

[77] When the losing player obtains more games in the first set than in the second, this is often, *but not always*, a sign that he or she has given up.

- Right at the moment, isn't it just more comfortable to let a match take its own course? You feel bad for a while if you lose, but when you look back at your match, you can even rationalize a victory: "I could have, might have, should have…"

- Care? How much do we care about what is right? If someone cheats us, do we challenge their call, or are we afraid to make waves? If we are mistakenly served a diet Coke rather than a regular coke in a restaurant, do we ask for what we want, or are we afraid to make waves?

- These days, Ali does not challenge ball calls or fight for the correct score when playing since she doesn't care, doesn't concentrate. In tennis terms, she's in a funk.

- Ali continually re-thinks her strokes during a match to subconsciously rationalize the fact that if she loses, she can point to a technical "practice" problem rather than worrying about a minor detail like "winning."

- Losing players hang out with others[78] who have already abandoned the game in their heads and don't want to fight for what is really theirs.

- Does this faith, fight, grit, *gnaque* (French), *grinta* (Italian), fighting spirit come from religion, and can one do well without it? In 1989, Michael Chang invoked Jesus in winning the French Open.

- What is missing in former top player Dinara Safina's inability to play really well when the Championship is on the line? Where is Safina today?[79]

And, not to make any comparisons, where is my daughter today?

---

[78] My definition of a *loser* is one who doesn't care, doesn't fight, and doesn't give all he can to something yet continues to indulge himself grudgingly in the activity. It is not someone who fights like hell and happens to lose. A close well-fought match is a win-win for everyone concerned.

[79] In 2011, Safina basically retired due to back problems.

Since I am an eternal optimist when it comes to tennis, I rationalize that she will come out of this psychologically stronger. She has an excellent tennis level, she is still young, and she will find out what she wants to do one day. However, in the competitive tennis world today, I realize that she probably won't scale the great heights she really could ascend to without a total attitude makeover.

Therein lies the rub.

I have always tried to be pro-active rather than reactive. I'm afraid that ten years from now, she will look back to 2009 and say, "I could have been a contender, and I really wasn't that far off."

I do not want her to look back when it's too late, but this really is for her to decide.

In this respect, it makes sense for her to take a step back this summer, ask, "What do I really want?" and then figure it out.

What I fear right now is that she will take the easy way out and not strive for anything, be it in school or on the court.

But this is for her to decide.

I have to remain optimistic that the excellent psychologist she saw only a few times at the beginning of the summer will help her find her way.

August 10, 2009

Ali did the *Campionnati Sardi* three weeks ago with a semi-final finish in singles (losing to Francesca P in three sets 7-6, 3-6, 1-6).[80] She also went to the finals in mixed with Simone and to the semis in women's doubles.

Ali was expected to win the tournament this year against Elisa S, who beat her in last year's final (even though Ali had significant leads in both sets). But Elisa was not even expected to get close to Ali this time around. Nevertheless, Elisa went on to squash Francesca P, 6-1, 6-2, in the final round, and as of this writing (2011), has won the past four years.

Because of Ali's dismissive attitude, I did not even go to see Ali's matches or comment on any of them. Nor did I comment on the cups that she won in singles and mixed doubles.

I am disappointed in her, not for her loss in the semi-finals (which is what she thinks) but in her nonchalant attitude. She continues to go downhill, in my estimation, and cares only about social activity. Some people would look at me and say, "Hey, give her a break. She's just a normal kid! What were you like when you were her age?" Answer: At her age, I was interested in tennis and school. It was later that I became more social.

She has become a spectator, a watcher, a follower—not a doer. What she is interested in—pop music to an obsession, looking good and being cool—I don't give a damn about.

We are having a much easier summer since there are no daily trips to the Geovillage tennis center, and there are no more tournaments to plan for. Still, I can't wait for September because she will have to go back to the physiotherapist for her back, the psychologist for her temperament, and will presumably enroll in a tennis club. We'll see.

Where are you going now, tennis player?

---

[80] Notice Ali's diminishing score line, in red, from set to set.

November 2009

After two months back, Ali is behind in her studies and playing limited tennis but regularly sees an excellent psychologist. Ali is also enrolled in a posture and exercise program that is top-notch to my mind. She goes twice a week for two hours as well as every day during the school vacations. She sees the psychologist once a week.

These two things are really helping her.

I have met with the psychologist who seems to be very kind and knows her business: Ali has made rational progress with her, and as long as I—DAD!!—keep out of the way, not talk about tennis and keep a distance, we get along.

The tennis club in Paris that she's in is excellent, and she has a coach who is extremely taken with physical fitness and posture. Due to her scoliosis, Ali's posture has always been weak since she was a child and this new coach noticed this right away.

To the coach's credit, he is the one who urged Ali to join the posture class.

To my credit, I have been on Ali's case ever since she was a little girl to keep her back straight.

To Ali's credit, she has taken this posture and stretching class very seriously.

After all these years, she has finally understood that she needs to stand straight, and I couldn't agree more.

It seems that my personal and professional success is very important for her. At least this is what the psychologist feels—not only does she have to deal with her own psychological improvement, mine has to develop hand in hand. I'm starting to feel that she looks at my success as just—or more important—than her own to the point that if I don't succeed at what I do, she has an excuse not to succeed as well. This I disagree with in theory, although, in practice, it has lit a fire under my butt to do better work and bring my own projects to completion. I guess the message I have to retain is that I can't complain about anything having to do with me, i.e., I must have no worries about money, spending, and I must make sure that everything's perfect so that she can feel enclosed in her own little bubble, and especially in her tennis bubble. As the strong, loud type, I will have to take on all these problems silently!

As for tennis, and to finish out her 2008-09 French tennis season,[81] she had a terrible September and five poor tournaments. She pulled out of two because she was not ready, lost in the first round of two others against lower-ranked players, and lost in the second round at St. Julien to a highly ranked -15 player who happened to not be that good. She finished the season with a 0 ranking, thereby losing one French ranking level from 2007-08.

---

[81] The French tennis season ends on October 1st.

The good news is that even though she's playing less, she's still playing, and I feel that if she does come back to play professionally, she'll go the whole hog. I think she'll at least play college tennis, and I think she'll do this in the right spirit of things. That being said, however, I've been ordered to lose interest in what she's up to and back out of her life. Maybe what she and her psychologist have told me is having its effect?

Actually, this is not entirely true as here I am sitting in my car wondering how she's doing in a *"contre"*[82]—a match that she should win—because she's playing a lower-ranked girl. I'm sitting in my car because I am not allowed to watch her, but if I do watch and she loses, she goes apeshit. If she wins, she also goes apeshit because I didn't do what she wanted me to. So now I'm the taxi driver and have to wait until she talks to me. I do this because this is my daughter, and I put her success above all. If or when she fails to be the best she can be, she'll never be able to turn around and say that I kept her from winning. She'll always be forced to say that I did my best for her. In my childish way, I never want her to be able to say that I was not there for her. If I had refused to drive her, then she would have been able to say that I didn't help her as much as I could have even though all I've ever done really is tried to help her. Therefore, two fantasies are possible and one reality probable:

Positive Fantasy 1: That she becomes a pro and that I'll reap the glory for having started her out and pushed her to work with the best. This scenario is almost null and void.

---

[82] In French, a *"contre"* is a match against someone ranked lower than you are. It is the opposite of a "perf" or "performance," a win against someone more highly ranked than you are.

Negative Fantasy 2: She becomes a tennis dropout and says, "I could have been a contender." This is not as satisfying as the first possibility in that it is more or less of an "I told you so" phenomenon—I told you to work harder, play more, do this, be that, etc.

Probable Reality: The reality is that she'll probably do ok enough to get through college and play tennis for four years with a scholarship. When she gets through, she'll probably study communication and psychology or go into some sort of fashion marketing.

The Tennis Bubble

CHAPTER 7

Bonte's Bests

To conclude, I'd like to write down some of the sayings and clichés I've heard over many years, most of which I've used on the court. I've even made some of them up:

1) Tennis is Life. All the rest is mere details.
2) The Law of Mankind: Many are called, but few are chosen.
3) Show me a good loser, and I'll show you a loser.
4) Tennis mirrors life.
5) A saying is nothing compared to tennis when it comes to learning life's lessons, e.g., I can tell you 'til I'm blue in the face that if you keep running up against the other girl's strength, you will eventually get burned. If you exploit her weakness, you will invariably prosper. But telling you is nothing compared to actually playing to a girl's strength and losing or pounding an opponent's weakness and winning.
6) Winning tennis will be the final judge.
7) Rules are meant to help and challenge you.
8) It's showtime!
9) On cheating, Part I: Always be honest, but if you're being played for a sucker, don't just put up with the other girl's cheating! Cheat right back but don't do it surreptitiously. Call the next ball struck in the middle of the court with a loud "OUT!" That will stop the cheating right there in its tracks.

The Tennis Bubble

10) On cheating, Part II: If there's a problem, don't move, stop playing, and don't say anything. Let the other guy call the referee. Silence is golden. (I learned this on the tennis court from my very young son who would not move until his opponent overturned his own cheating call!)
11) Learn from failure.
12) You can't get better without a goal.
13) Learn how to be alone out there: Do it by yourself.
14) Go beyond yourself. Extend your limits.
15) As Kipling says in "If"—"Fill the unforgiving minute with sixty seconds worth of distance run."
16) Or, as he also says: "If you can meet with Triumph [winning] and Disaster [losing] and treat those two imposters just the same ..."[83]
17) Be the captain of your ship and see what it involves.
18) Is tennis an end in itself?

---

[83] "Winning" and "losing" reflect my personal interpretation.

The Tennis Bubble

EPILOGUE

It is now the late fall of 2011, and Ali is doing well in both her studies and tennis. She is a happy sophomore with a major in Communication.

She finished her first year of college with a 3.68 GPA, mainly scoring A's and a few B's, an excellent result.

She has made a lot of friends and seems much more mature than before.

She has finished the first leg of a four-year, "full-ride" athletic scholarship and is now halfway through another year.

She still plays tennis three hours a day, had a respectable win-loss record throughout her freshman year on the women's tennis team and now regularly qualifies for ITFs. For these, she is not allowed to accept any prize money except that which covers tournament expenses.

She works very hard on her game and plays only for herself and no longer for us. If she loses, it's not my fault, her coach's fault, or anyone else's. It's her responsibility, just like when she wins.

She now realizes where she stands—not only in tennis but in life—and wants to finish her B.A. in Communication and earn a master's degree.

Depending on her results, she may or may not want to play professional tennis full-time after college.

As for the rest, she's got her whole life in front of her, and all the doors are wide open.

What more could anyone ask for?

I'm very proud of her.

The Tennis Bubble

Alessandra at USF, Tampa

Footnotes

1.   I often refer to the Nick Bollettieri Tennis Academy as *"NBTA, The Academy* or just *Bollettieri"* in this book.

2.   IMG, the top sports agency in the world at the time, had bought out the Chris Evert and Nick Bollettieri names, putting the Evert Academy on the East (Boca Raton), and the Bollettieri Academy on the West coast (Bradenton).

3.   I have mostly used the pronouns "he" and "him" to refer *in general* to children or people even though I spend most of the book talking about my daughter. In addition to "you," I sometimes even use "she" and "her" when I'm speaking generally. However, I see no obligation to employ a female pronoun to speak about *mankind,* a neutral word used for hundreds of years to refer to both men and women. I eschew the politically correct terms "womankind" or "humankind," priggish words brought into the English language by do-gooders and fops desirous of selling their sexist agenda or intent on wanting us all to languish in tepid and insipid egalitarianism.

4.   The French have a complicated way of ranking tennis players but it is much more accurate than its American equivalent in that one knows the ability of a player just by his ranking, provided the player has been playing continuously and competitively for a few months at least:

- Players start off non-ranked in the bottom of the fourth division (bottom of the pyramid) and move up through the divisions to the first division (top of the pyramid). Some eventually make it up to the "promo" (promotion) or top national ranking and then they are numbered 1-50. (Top French pros like Gael Monfils or Jo-Wilfried Tsonga would be in the top five players, for example.)

- The origin of ranking categories like "30/4, 15/2, or 2/6" stems from the handicap system: A player who is better than another might "give" 2 points (30) for four games to another, or in the case of 15/2, he might "grant" 1 point (15) for two sets to another. Today, handicaps are not observed but the ranking system remains: the lower the ranking number a player has in France, the stronger he is.

5. Aside from Alessandra, the three of us in the family are right-handed and left-lateralized. Ali is the other way: left-handed and right lateralized. Most of us have one dominant right or left hand and foot. However, lateralization refers to what side one prefers using while doing many different tasks that don't necessarily require a dominant hand or foot, e.g., picking things out of a car, riding a scooter, sweeping the floor, buttoning one's shirt, etc.

6. Louis XIV was born in 1638 in a large chateau that was first built by Louis VI in 1122 and had served Kings and Queens ever since. Later on, after Louis XIV had removed to Versailles, he would continue to return to his birthplace and 'country cottage' chateau where he would start his hunts down into the Valley of the Seine and across the forest of Le Vésinet (where we moved three and a half centuries later in 1998).

7. In France, every eight weeks of classes is followed by two weeks of school holiday.

8. At the time, she attended school four days a week like other French children except one morning and afternoon per week (one day total) were exclusively set aside for British instruction for native English speakers.

The Tennis Bubble

9.   Michael Llodra's and Fabrice Santoro's former coach and (last I heard) the coach of up-and-coming French stars, Guillaume Rufin, Axel Michon and (much later on) Luca Pouille.

10.   Max(imilian) Bonte was born in May 2002.

11. Since then, his hourly rate doubled in less than five years and now I don't know what it is.

12. Chip was top-tenner Jelena Jankovic's coach throughout 2010.

13. During these boom times (2003-4), the numbers were always getting higher and it was common knowledge that the Bollettieri Academy just wanted your money.

14. Someone once told me golf was the toughest. Maybe it is, mentally. I wouldn't know except to say that it doesn't compare—physically—to tennis.

15. Note that most of these journal notes reflect my point of view ***at the time of writing*** (2005-8) and have not been "re-spun" to correspond to what I know now (2021).

16. Apparently, this owner was a big finance guy and had become a loner and—although completely dedicated to his three sons—had accumulated so much debt that he took his own life in our bedroom. When we arrived, there was a bullet hole in one of the floor tiles. Some handyman mentioned that a hanging plant in a heavy pot had fallen on this tile but I didn't believe him. The former owner's blue suit was in the closet, and the rest of the apartment was painted a muddy, brown color and reflected African themes.

17. Facebook hadn't reached its zenith yet.

18. In all fairness, Europe has become only *slightly* more consumer-friendly than what it used to be.

19. In 2005-6, Amelie Mauresmo was a top-ten player in the world.

20. **Super Series**: the more highly rated local junior tournaments. **Sectionals**: more highly rated junior tournaments which involve that section of the country where one lives (Southeast Florida, Northeast, etc.). **Nationals**: like the name implies, junior tournaments played at the USTA national level divided up into gender and age categories. **ITF**: International Tennis Federation tournaments which give one ITF junior or ATP (men's) or WTA (women's) points depending on the dollar amount of the ITF, the age of the player and whether that player accepts prize money or not. College players aren't supposed to accept any prize money except that which covers their expenses.

21. Whether in France or in Florida…

22. Accent Reduction involves "reducing" one's foreign accent in English by rendering it more understandable to the native English speaker's ear—any variety of English.

23. A sturdy metal cane with a small leather seat that can be used alternatively as a walking stick or a seat to watch sporting events.

24. The two-handed backhand came into wide use with Bjorn Borg in the 1970s and initially was a more consistent, powerful shot that was easier to impart topspin to the ball than the one-handed backhand. This was because the non-dominant hand created the top spin. Despite gains in racquet-making technology (racquets are lighter), many children still play with the two-hander today because they start so young and don't have the strength to swing a racquet with one hand on their backhand side. At the end of the day, however, one can do a lot more with the one-handed backhand, including imparting top spin.

25. Nanny Jocelyne died in 2013.

26. The Stanley Cup is the premier prize for ice hockey in North America. After a long hockey season lasting from early

September through late March, sixteen teams take to the ice for the playoffs, which last another two months for the winning team to emerge and take the Stanley Cup.

27. Carling gave birth to a fourth child in 2010 and a fifth in 2011!!

28. From 2006-2011, she also used the following tennis teachers: 32) Warren, the Australian Lefty -- 33) Yuri -- 34) Jose L -- 35) Sylvester (Sly) B -- 36) Giorgio B -- 37) Simone M -- 38) Isabelle G -- 39) Jean-Marie -- 40) Gilles D - - 41) Agustin M -- 42) Yuri -- 43) Irena.

29. Just to put the record straight, 100% is certainly not a level I ever reached in my matches although I did play at 90% from time to time.

30. I only improved this part of my game later on in life. Yoga and psychotherapy helped a lot.

31. From July 2005 to July 2008, Ali had to wear a back brace to stabilize her scoliosis during her adolescent and growth years.

32. Rob S, former top 20 player in singles and number one doubles player in the world (with Ken F) is married to Carling S.

33. Renowned claycourter Guillermo P-R, formerly 13 in the world, worked with my daughter (mostly in the summers) from 2003-2009.

34. NBTA regularly schedules weekend "Grand Prix" tournaments which give points to the participants and which culminate in a "Grand Prix Masters" event at the end of May.

35. Angela Maria Lopera was a good player and coach who had had a lot of influence at Bollettieri.

36. Thanks to Lance L, the Bollettieri Academy has cameras installed on every court so that one can review any match one wants to.

37. 'rich people's problems'

38. A "back draw" is a consolation draw for first round main draw losers.

39. Originally in English but translated into many languages, "Spotty" is a cartoon dog series where Spotty is about the age of a five-year-old child.

40. I am not happy with her breaking her racquet. I am happy that she cares enough to want to win.

41. From "If" by Rudyard Kipling

42. Lance L produced a few "winning DVDs" in which he isolates Ali's winners from previously recorded matches. The idea is to watch one of these before going out on the court before a match and get "psyched-up."

43. Held on the Bollettieri Academy courts.

44. I wrote them a note but like everything today, it was never answered. It was as if I had never spoken—a lone voice baying for naught to the wind.

45. If the USTA or any other tennis organization used local children, retirees or other volunteers/club members *to sit in the umpire's chair* and referee a match—and paid them minimally—a lot of this cheating would go away. Official retired USTA referees who are paid $150-$200 a day to walk around the different courts usually arrive **after** the cheating has occurred.

46. One of Ali's Ukrainian tennis friends

47. This coach had been particularly impressed with my daughter when he had seen her play in another tournament.

48. *Train Grande Vitesse*=High speed train

49. Jean Bouin is the name of a club in Paris which also houses the "Lagardere" group (top French players like Richard Gasquet and Michael LLodra belong to this group).

50. *"Remettre les pendules à l'heure"*

51. Percy M also rented different places he had bought out to the parents of players. Maybe he was trying to steal back some of my business after I had stolen his?

52. *Eye-Eye* E was a very nice girl about Ali's age who had suffered physical setbacks but who also possessed a terrific work ethic to compensate for them. I was never sure about the spelling of her name.

53. An International Tennis Federation junior tournament played for points, not money.

54. Junior ITFs start off at the bottom level Grade 5s and work up to the tough Grade 1s.

55. Pendleton is the K-12th grade school on the Bollettieri Academy

56. Still very young today, Nicole V was top 20 in the world in 2007.

57. These are obviously my tongue-in-cheek rules for dealing with many but not all tennis parents.

58. Cristina, a real user, had been a thorn in our side in the Guadalajara tournament ITF last January 2007. Nevertheless, Ali was still friends with her.

59. Centre National d'Education: France's National Education Center correspondence studies program

60. International Performance Institute is another term for hard exercise!

61. Looking at this schedule now, with hindsight, I can see why she wanted to be on MSN. This was a killer schedule!

62. I later wrote a note to the USTA detailing my plan but, as usual, was completely ignored.

63. Notre Dame de Grace, a predominantly French-Canadian district in Montreal.

64. "El Loco'" means "the nut case."

65. For every winner she hits, she hits two losers

66. Now 15, Q is 82 ITF juniors in March 2011

67. Internal Grand Prix and related tournaments are organized regularly at the NBTA throughout the year.

68. Strings lose 8 to 10% of their tension within a few hours of stringing.

69. Nine out of ten tennis players play right-handed.

70. According to the sports clipping in the local paper, Ali was currently #522 and M-F B, #466 ITF.

71. God knows that these fundamentals were taught over and over again. It just goes to show that it is not what is taught but what is retained that is the answer and this is why so many are called and so few are chosen.

72. Mind you, had Ali established a winning record and/or dramatically improved her tennis, she might not have been so attracted by this alternative social life. Does winning solve all problems? No, but it helps!

73. John E and Johan K were a top South African 1980s doubles team and both excellent singles players in their own right. Only about 5'8", Johan K went as high as number 7 in the world. John and Johan both started an Academy in Longboat Key but then went their separate ways in the Tampa Bay area.

74. There are certain people who stigmatize the use of this term "Plan B" as in "everyone has to have a Plan B." The feeling is, "if you have to have a Plan B, then you don't have enough of a Plan A." Real champions don't have a Plan B. They roar straight ahead to Plan A. Furthermore, these people feel that admitting the existence of a Plan B is tantamount to being a loser. My feeling is that even the number 1 men and women's players in the world didn't spend their whole day playing tennis on their way up and

they all needed some career after the age of thirty so maybe we need to call Plan B, *Plan A+*.

75. Tiffany D originally wanted to live with us in France and go to tournaments with Ali. However, the chemistry between Ali and Tiffany wasn't the best.

76. Pronounced "Si-<u>mown</u>-ay".

77. When the losing player obtains more games in the first set than in the second, this is sometimes, *but not always*, a sign that he or she has given up.

78. My definition of a *loser* is one who doesn't care, doesn't fight, and doesn't give all he can to something yet continues to indulge himself grudgingly in the activity. It is not someone who fights like hell and happens to lose. A close well-fought match is a win-win for everyone concerned.

79. In 2011, Safina basically retired due to back problems.

80. Notice Ali's diminishing score line, in red, from set to set.

81. The French tennis season ends on October 1st.

82. In French, a *"contre"* is a match against someone ranked lower than you are. It is the opposite of a "perf" or "performance," a win against someone more highly ranked than you are.

83. "Winning" and "losing" reflect my personal interpretation.

The Tennis Bubble

ALSO BY RICHARD BONTE:

Novels by Richard Bonte & James Crew Allen

Grand Cayman, Exposed

The Wuhan Tentacles

The Baja Redemption

Novellas by
Richard Bonte & James Crew Allen

The Second Promised Land (Baja Redemption Book Two)

A Pact with the Devil

Novella by Richard Bonte

Skeletons in the Closet

Novella by Richard Bonte and David G. Lee

I will "Prey" for You, My Love

Novels by Richard Bonte & Hamilton Harcourt Fleming III

Black on White: The Roaring Twenties

All Black: 1930's Hollywood Secret Lives

The Three Cousins

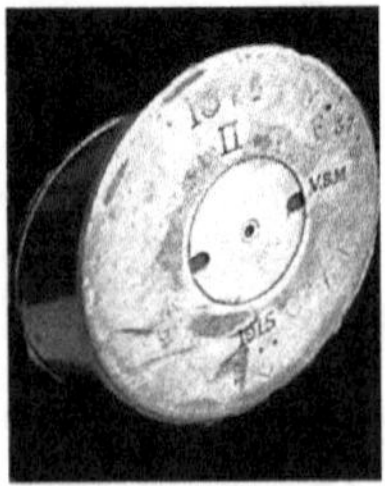

Novels by Richard Bonte & Jayne Louise Cramforde

The Sisters

Sisters

Sisters by Bonte&Cramforde, PRINT&E-BOOK

Novels by Richard Bonte

Curmudgeonly Yours

Terry's Upside

Against Nature: Waste

The Tennis Bubble

Short Stories by Richard Bonte

Curmudgeon in McDonald's

From Muslimia to Tattooland

The Tennis Bubble

The Tattooed Server

The Choice

Short Plays by Richard Bonte

The Empire One-Act

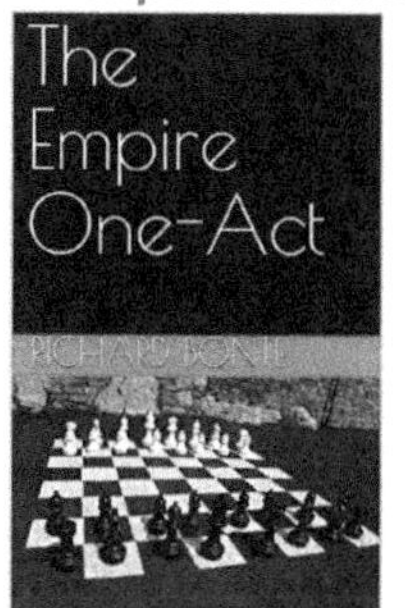

Smarter Than You: Trump Derangement Syndrome Run Amok